Thank It's God Monday

Thank God It's Monday

Celebrating Your Purpose at **Work**

Kim Hackney

Baker Books

A Division of Baker Book House Co
Grand Rapids, Michigan 49516

Published by Baker Books
a division of Baker Book House Company
P.O. Box 6287, Grand Rapids, MI 49516-6287
www.bakerbooks.com

Printed in the United States of America

Library of Congress Cataloging-in-Publication Data
Hackney, Kim, 1963–
      Thank God it's Monday : celebrating your purpose at work / Kim Hackney.
            p.   cm.
      Includes bibliographical references.
      ISBN 0-8010-6433-3 (pbk.)
      1. Christian women—Religious life. 2. Christian life—Biblical teaching. I.
Title.
BV4527.H33 2003
248.8′43—dc21   2003004223

To my husband, sweetie, and true love, Kevin.
I thank God upon every remembrance of you.
You are more than I ever dreamed of and more than
I can ever acknowledge. I love you!

Acknowledgments

To the many people who have encouraged me, uplifted me, and interceded for me during this season of my life, I pray God's great and lavish blessings in your life! Thank you Pat Dixon for continually praying Scripture over my life; Noelene Goodman for counseling me in wisdom; Tracey Mixon for being my everyday girlfriend; Laryssa Toomer for challenging me to walk in truth; and Tiffany Williams for being my faithful sister-in-love. To Chloe Gooden, Chris Malkemes, Becky Robateau, Audra Roper, and Marj Stephens, thank you for sowing prayers into this vision when it was still in the proposal stages.

Thank you Heart of America Christian Writers' Network group for welcoming me as one of your own. You have been a vehicle of truth and inspiration for me as a writer and speaker. No matter where I live, you will always have my heart (and membership!).

Jo Kadlecek, thank you for leading me to Bob Hosack and the staff at Baker Books—as you indicated, a perfect match! To my patient and gracious editor Vicki Crumpton, thank you for seeing the vision and holding it dear to your heart . . . blessings upon blessings to you.

To my family, I am deeply indebted to you. Kevin, thank you for extending to me the "gift of time," without complaining, so I could immerse myself in this vision. To my beloved children, Candace, Christian, and Cyrus, thank you for your overflowing love, laughter, and joy. You are my encouragement.

And of course praise and honor and glory to the one true God, whose one word in my life has been translated into a thousand more on these pages, consuming everything I am. Thank you for using me—the least likely—to bring forth your Word.

Soli Deo Gloria!

Introduction

Victorious living! That's what this book is all about. As I thought about this, my mind raced back to a time when I visited a family member in prison. I recalled the heaviness of the emotions that engulfed me as the prison guard opened the steel frame doors, patted me down, and then led me to the prison courtyard, where I anxiously waited for what seemed like hours. There I pondered the proverbial question, "How could my beloved end up here?" A prisoner, in chains!

If you have a relative or friend in prison, you know exactly what I'm talking about. We are constantly asking why and how. The same types of questions about my work plagued me for years, making me feel like a prisoner in my workplace.

Have you ever struggled to make sense of your workplace ... your purpose ... your reason for being ... your feelings of captivity? I have! For years I felt like a prisoner with no hope. I dreaded Monday mornings and counted the hours to the close of business on Fridays. Yet as a Christian I knew there had to be more to my workweek than my title, position, or paycheck. Indeed there is, and this is what I want to share and encourage you with: God's purpose.

11

In the first two chapters we will uncover the world's hollow and deceptive philosophy, which often takes us captive and imprisons us with the desire for more power, possessions, and prestige. We'll replace this lie with God's truth. I pray that as God's truths are unfolded for you, you will learn what it means to be "prosperous and successful" in your workplace.

Chapters 3, 4, and 5 will encourage you to be a woman of noble character, to communicate heart to heart, and to overcome the workplace conflict that is often part of day-to-day interactions with others. We will learn from the life of Ruth what a woman of noble character looks like in the workplace, from the apostle Paul how to be an effective and relevant communicator, and from various biblical characters how to triumph over conflict with God's Word.

Only as we live victoriously in these areas can we bear witness to the power of Jesus in our lives so others are drawn to him. This is the focus of chapter 6: sharing your personal testimony—the Good News of Jesus in your life—and understanding the importance of encouraging one another as believers in the workplace.

We all deserve to be valued in the workplace. However, this does not always happen, as we see in chapter 7. This chapter takes an honest look at discrimination and harassment in the workplace and gives practical and spiritual guidance for overcoming these painful workplace situations.

The last two chapters are about seeking and celebrating God in your life. Specifically, chapter 8 addresses seeking God before venturing out into a new job or career opportunity. And chapter 9 is our celebration chapter, focusing on what it means to honor God with your life.

God wants us to live in complete victory, including in the workplace. To do this, however, we must tear down the pervasive lies of the enemy and not be taken captive by the world's philosophy of success. As 1 John 2:15–17 tells us, "Do not love the world or anything in the world. If anyone loves the world, the love of the Father is not in him. For everything in the world—the cravings of sinful man, the lust of his eyes and the boasting of what he has and does—comes not from the Father but from the world. The world and its desires pass away, but the man who does the will of God lives forever."

Only as we start living according to God's Word and renewing our minds on his truth will we be able to tear down the walls that are holding us captive in the workplace.

If you are ready to be set free, then know that the great and mighty Lord has personally summoned and equipped you to begin celebrating your purpose at work!

Like you, I bought into the idea of "TGIF" for many years and often have to fight against that attitude now. This seemingly harmless attitude is contrary to God's Word and eats away at us spiritually, emotionally, mentally, and physically. Let me explain.

Flash back to quitting time on a Friday afternoon. You've just escaped, and you're officially on the other side of the prison walls called *work*. You get in your car, turn on the music, and head for home. As you open the door, you sigh, "Thank God it's Friday!" You settle down and then get something to eat. Exhausted from the day, you slump down on the couch in an attempt to relax. There you spend the remainder of the evening replaying the past stresses of the week.

Finally you relax, but it's time for bed. You sleep for what seems like five minutes and then hit the ground running first thing Saturday. Saturday comes and goes like the speed of light. Your only nagging thought is, "Ugh, work is only one day away!"

It's Sunday! You roll over one last time and can hardly believe it's already time for church, and then you suddenly shudder at the thought of work—*tomorrow!* Instead of listening to the well-prepared sermon, you are softly crying out inside, "Lord, please prepare me for the week ahead." And while everyone thinks you've been moved by the pastor's heartfelt message, you know better! Sunday draws to an end, and you slowly go into a slight depression, praying for strength to get you through *another* week.

Monday comes and you pray, "Lord, just get me through to Wednesday." Wednesday arrives and you anticipate Friday, knowing it's only two more days until the great escape. Friday's here and you yell, "Thank God it's Friday!" And then the vicious cycle starts again!

See what a little harmless attitude can do? If we believe we are working for the Lord, we see our workweek as an opportunity to serve him. If not, we think of work merely as a means to make money, gain status, or put in our time. Isn't it just like the enemy to try to deceive us with this small but important attitude? He knows that if this TGIF attitude can prevail in our life, we will miss the opportunity to minister to those we are around most.

Society embraces this TGIF mentality with a smile and happy hour, but I can't help but believe it grieves God. Not only are we using God's name irreverently and flippantly, but we have bought into the world's hollow philosophy instead of what God has for us.

If you've been in the workplace longer than a nanosecond, you can probably relate to and see through this subtle yet pervasive lie of the enemy. This is just one of the many lies the enemy wants us to embrace so our lives are stripped of God's joy, peace, and victory in the workplace. Despite the enemy's attempt to take ministry out of our forty-hour-plus workweek, I bring you good news—God's Word! John 10:10 tells us that Christ came to give us life in abundance. This is God's plan for our lives. It's his desire that we experience his abundance, and that includes abundance in our workplace.

During the remainder of this chapter we will discuss seven other lies the enemy uses to keep us living in defeat and hopelessness in the workplace. My prayer for you is that as God's truth is revealed you are excited in spirit, encouraged by truth, equipped to withstand the enemy's schemes, and ultimately ready to experience victory in the workplace. If you will, keep an open heart as we begin to tear down the world's hollow and deceptive philosophy.

17

Placing Work before God

"Lord, I promise, tomorrow!" Tomorrow comes and you sheepishly whisper once again, "Lord, I promise, tomorrow!" Then after months of promising God "tomorrow," you resign yourself to the fact that you are just too busy, especially with your crazy work schedule, to spend time in prayer or in the Bible. "After all," you reason, "God gave me this job and he knows better than anyone the unreasonable demands and time constraints being placed on me. Right?"

Have you ever felt this way? Well, this was my life for many, many years. The alarm clock would go off and I would begin my marathon day, racing against time. Then one day I shared my frustrations with a close friend. I opened my heart about my life revolving around my work and blurted out, "I haven't had a devotion in months!"

As I was speaking those words, the thought hit me: *Work is my life*. As a single woman striving for professional status, I had abandoned my first love, God, in pursuit of a fast-paced career in human resources. After listening to me, my dear friend Lina responded with something so simple yet profound that it changed my life. She said, "The only thing that keeps me sane is spending time in the Word of God. I am committed to devotional time every day!"

I remember being "wowed" that she spent daily time in the Word despite her hectic schedule. Honestly, this was revolutionary! I don't think I actually knew another professional who wasn't a minister or preacher who did something so radical.

As our conversation progressed we talked about the importance of spending time in the Word of God and the blessings, refreshment, and intimacy that came from this time. She encouraged me not to be so consumed with the day's events that those things took higher priority than my relationship with God. Years later, I see how her wisdom and encouragement have made me a stronger Christian woman.

God commands, "You shall have no other gods before me" (Deut. 5:7). He knows that when we place things before him, like our career, our focus gets blurred, foundational truths get uprooted, faith turns to fear, and a close relationship with him is something we can only reminisce about, leaving a deep void in our heart. Just look at the life of King Solomon. We know from Scripture that Solomon was a man with great riches, wealth, and wisdom. He appeared to have everything, but when he placed things before the Lord and succumbed to the lusts of this world, he broke his covenant with God and became filled with regret (see 1 Kings 11:6–13).

Pursuits outside of God are meaningless. Not until the end of Solomon's life did he find the true value of life and pen these words in Psalm 127:1: "Unless the LORD builds the house, its builders labor in vain."

Having a career is great—but placing it before God leads to a lonely road, often requiring us to forsake family, friends, and most importantly, our fellowship with God. The choice is so clear. We can either labor for the Lord and receive the blessings he has in store for us, or we can work our fingers to the bone, placing God on hold, striving aimlessly to be fulfilled by the false god called work.

God loves us so much that he beckons us to place him first so we can experience a relationship with him and reap the blessings and benefits of knowing him in our day-to-day commitment. Only as we place God in his rightful place, above all else, are we able to overcome the devil's schemes to keep us in workplace captivity.

If Only They Paid Me More

Money really is a necessity! No one would argue with that, and money in itself is not evil. But because society places such a high premium on money, it has become another form of idolatry. Our society has abandoned its founding truth of "In God We Trust" and placed its values and morality in the arms of money, hoping to achieve "the American dream."

Consider, for instance, the once-popular television show *Who Wants to Be a Millionaire?* With all the media attention that show received, most of us have either directly or indirectly been part of a conversation about what we would do with a million bucks. Personally, I've spent some time thinking, "If only . . ." Then one night I picked up the phone to hear, "Is this Kim Hackney? Kim, Bob has selected you to be part of 'Who Wants to Be a Millionaire?' You have sixty seconds to answer this question: 'What is the name of the Italian opera singer . . . ?'"

Of course it wasn't really the television host but a good friend whose family was playing the home version of the game as part of family night. Nonetheless, I was glad to have answered the question correctly and contributed to the "wealth" of this contestant. But if only it had been Regis!

Oops, this is what I'm talking about. "If only" thinking is so destructive to Christians because it takes our focus off God, places our faith in something besides God, and causes us to become impatient with trusting in God to meet all our needs. Could this be why God tells us, "You shall not make for yourself an idol in the form of anything in heaven above or on the earth beneath or in the waters below" (Deut. 5:8)?

As career women we need to guard our hearts against all forms of idolatry but especially against the god of money.

Whether it's money we are making, money we want to make, money in the family, or the money we keep pushing our husbands to make, we need to guard our hearts against greed. Society would like for us to believe that more money brings happiness, contentment, or peace, so we chase after it as though life itself depended on it. But as Christians we know that our life depends upon God and it's in him that we are given these internal blessings.

First Timothy 6:10 says, "For the love of money is a root of all kinds of evil. Some people, eager for money, have wandered from the faith and pierced themselves with many griefs." When we look to money to meet internal needs, as only God can do, we are making for ourselves an idol in the form of money. Since most people don't talk about idolatry anymore, we tend to dismiss its prominence in our lives, believing we are not susceptible to its snares.

Consider for a moment: Do you know people in the workplace who are always tying their "if only" happiness to money, power, possessions, or status and never seem content with what God has given them? This is deception at its best, because Satan often disguises our "if onlys" as ambition, when in reality it's greed! We can spot deception by asking a few hard but telling questions: "If I never get this raise, will I still trust God?" "If I'm overlooked for this position, will I continue to experience God's peace?" "Am I content with the blessings I have?"

Once in a while we all need to check ourselves and make sure we are not investing too much of our time, talent, and heart in things other than God. God has great riches in store for us, some of which will come in the form of financial or professional status and some in the form of internal benefits. Neither the external or internal blessings will ever come at the expense of our relationship with God. He wants our hearts completely surrendered to him, the one true God!

God Is My Witness, I Swear

"Yahweh" is a Hebrew name for God and means "I AM."[1] When we look to God, we experience him as the "I AM" in our lives. We are afforded great security by knowing that the God we seek, serve, and surrender our lives to is the great I AM of yesterday, today, and forever. When we need peace, we can trust that his name means I AM Peace. When we need love, we know his name means I AM Love. If we need hope, his name means I AM Hope. As we grasp the reality of calling God "Yahweh," we should be humbled at the mere mention of his name because it is so powerful and all-consuming.

In the past, names were an indication of your family's heritage and most likely the legacy you would leave. Throughout the Bible God changed individuals' names as a testament of his handprint on their lives. However, today most names have little significance. And because of our general indifference to names, we've taken a laissez-faire attitude with the Lord's name. We irreverently use his name in everyday conversations and think nothing of it.

For years I turned a deaf ear to "innocent" statements spoken by others as they interjected God's name in their conversations to express disbelief or frustration. Worse yet, I used these phrases myself. Because I had become spiritually numb to reverencing God's name, I winked at this heresy and remained in captivity.

Society's heart is cold to God's truth; therefore using his name in vain means nothing to most people. And in the workplace just about everything imaginable has been done to strip the truth of God or Jesus from our environment, a place in dire need of a Savior. Just think for a moment about the office party in December. Did the memorandum say "Christmas Party," or did it say "Holiday Party"? It's almost unimaginable to see the word "Christmas" typed on a corporate Christmas card. Society has become so politically correct that most people have taken Christ out of their conversation when talking about the birth or resurrection of Jesus—but not so "politically correct" that they stop using the name of God or Jesus Christ to "damn" someone.

The enemy has used the weapon of political correctness to the detriment of Christians in the workplace and called it workplace tolerance. We should never succumb to "political correctness" when the Lord's name is not being reverenced in the highest regard. The Lord is sovereign, and whenever we do not hold his name in the absolute highest regard, we are misusing his name. As Christians in the workplace we need to retune our spiritual antennas and honor the name before which "every knee should bow, in heaven and on earth and under the earth, and every tongue confess that Jesus Christ is Lord" (Phil. 2:10–11).

The next time we hear someone misusing the Lord's name, let's politely and lovingly ask them not to. As we are reminded in Job 38, God is the one who

laid the foundation of the earth
marked off its dimensions
shut up the sea behind doors
gives order to the morning
shows the dawn its place
shapes the earth like clay
sends lightning bolts on their way
tips over the water jars of the heavens
satisfies the hunger of the lions

23

provides food for the raven
has dominion over the earth
can raise his voice over the clouds
cuts the channel for the rain
journeyed to the springs of the sea
walked in the recesses of the deep

Remember, "Do not misuse the name of the LORD your God" (Deut. 5:11 NLT), because he is the great I AM!

Work Till You Drop

Have you ever known someone who works seven days a week, around the clock, juggling one full-time job and possibly one or two other jobs? If you know someone like this, you know that this person is most likely drained emotionally, spiritually, and physically. Working like this requires great personal sacrifices affecting all aspects of life, but the greatest loss is sacrificing time resting in the Lord.

I believe that when God gave us this great commandment, "Observe the Sabbath day by keeping it holy" (Deut. 5:12), his purpose was strictly to protect us. He wasn't being legalistic or trying to burden us with one more commitment to etch on our calendars or "to do" lists. No indeed! This commandment is quite the opposite of legalism, which is another form of bondage. God wants us to experience the liberating freedom that comes from basking in his presence.

Hebrews 4:1 says, "Therefore, since the promise of entering his rest still stands, let us be careful that none of you be found to have fallen short of it." God promises rest so that we may experience the wholeness that comes from being in his presence both now and eternally. The Sabbath commandment,

24

like all the others, speaks to the heart of God and his desire for an intimate relationship with us.

What an awesome thought to know God loves us so much that he beckons us to reserve a special time set apart to be with him, like a date. He knows our spirits, minds, and bodies can only be refreshed as we saturate ourselves with his presence. And contrary to popular belief that the Sabbath is a day of "self-rest" (playing golf, going shopping at the mall, or lounging around the house in pajamas), I believe the rest God offers us is a life-changing rest. It's utterly impossible to be in God's presence and not come away extravagantly refreshed, renewed, and rested.

The writer of Hebrews teaches us the importance of Sabbath-resting in the Lord: "There remains, then, a Sabbath-rest for the people of God; for anyone who enters God's rest also rests from his own work, just as God did from his. Let us, therefore, make every effort to enter that rest, so that no one will fall by following [the Israelites'] example of disobedience. For the word of God is living and active. Sharper than any double-edged sword, it penetrates even to dividing soul and spirit, joints and marrow; it judges the thoughts and attitudes of the heart" (Heb. 4:9–12).

Awesome! This day of rest is for spiritual revival and physical reprieve. Only when we are resting in his presence are we able to operate in the Word of God, which is "living and active" and "sharper than any double-edged sword." What life-changing truth to know that as we rest in God's presence we are able to discern truth from darkness, morality from immorality, and good from evil. The reward of keeping the Sabbath equips us to be victorious in all aspects of our life. What matters most is that we consistently set aside time, apart from our normal work schedule, to rest in God's presence by keeping this day holy.

salary increase, bonus, or promotion? Consider this story of an employee who worked faithfully for a particular employer for over twenty years, was cheated in wages, and never received a promotion. Through the efforts of this man's hard work, his boss became a very wealthy man. The story goes something like this.

Jacob worked long, hard hours taking care of his boss's property, livestock, and household goods. With his excellent management skills, strong work ethic, and loyalty, Jacob multiplied his employer's business and family wealth to great proportions. After twenty years of being mistreated, lied to, and manipulated, Jacob decided to leave his place of employment. However, his boss was unwilling to give him his rightfully earned severance package and pension plan or any other form of compensation.

Jacob sought counsel and was told he could leave with a portion of his employer's wealth, livestock, and goods. However, Jacob's wife felt as though they'd been cheated out of an "inheritance." She took matters into her own hands. Instead of seeking counsel like Jacob did, she did what she deemed necessary, stealing something extremely valuable from the employer's house. Within days the employer noticed this valuable item missing and sought to settle the matter and vindicate himself by going after Jacob's family.

After reading this story do you feel the wife is justified? Can you see yourself ever doing anything like the wife? And how does the command "You shall not steal" (Deut. 5:19) fit into this situation? I confess, I've acted similarly to the wife mentioned in this biblical story of Jacob and Rachel (see Genesis 31), and maybe you have also. Have you ever taken a stapler without replacing it? What about taking a box of paper clips from your employer's office to do some home filing? Did you feel justified for one reason or another? Would your employer consider this stealing? Or if someone worked for you, would you consider these actions stealing?

Recently a radio show was giving statistics on employee theft. The host said companies are seeing financial losses in the millions each year due to employee theft. That's a lot of paper clips! But the devil, the father of lies, deceives us into rationalizing our behavior. Have you ever thought, "As hard as I work and the way they treat me, they are lucky this is all I'm taking"? What about, "As much money as this company makes off me, they'll never miss it"? Or simply, "I deserve it"?

Even though I can relate to Rachel's justifiable anger, in an attempt to get what was "rightfully" owed, she compromised her values and her family's safety as we read later in Genesis 31. In the workplace we must obey God's command, "Do not repay evil with evil or insult with insult, but with blessing, because to this you were called so that you may inherit a blessing" (1 Peter 3:9). In spite of how we feel or how passively society reacts to stealing something "small," we must take hold of God's Word, "You shall not steal" (Deut. 5:19), and let his truth prevail in our life.

Tell Them I'm Not Here

Sometimes you just have to tell a "white lie," don't you agree? If someone asked me this question a couple of years ago, I would have responded, "Well, it depends!" After all, society tells us it's okay to lie as long as it's a white lie. And believe it or not, there's actually a definition in the dictionary for white lie: "a minor lie uttered from polite, amiable, or pardonable motives; a polite or harmless fib."[3]

Isn't it interesting that I found a definition for "white lie" in the dictionary, but I couldn't find anything in the Bible? I was, however, able to find Scripture that says, "You shall not give false testimony" (Deut. 5:20) and "Do not lie" (Lev. 19:11). How is it that we have bought into this idea of a "white" lie?

Matthew 12:36–37 says, "Men will have to give account on the day of judgment for every careless word they have spoken. For by your words you will be acquitted, and by your words you will be condemned." These are the words spoken by Jesus. Therefore, no matter how we try to dress up the word *lie,* it still comes down to sin.

We've already established that Satan is the father of deception. When we lie we give him authority in our situation and over our tongue. I can recall many incidents in the workplace where I gave the enemy authority over my situation by lying instead of telling the truth and trusting God to work out my situation. Maybe you have been in a similar situation.

It was yet another hectic day in the office. I was quickly preparing for another meeting—probably the second or third one of the day—when I heard the phone ring and quickly said, "If it's for me, take a message. I'm not here." As soon as I uttered those words, I gave the devil authority over my tongue, my heart, and that situation. Not only did I lie, but I caused an employee under my authority to lie.

Each time we do something like this, we compromise our character and gradually destroy our testimony to the onlooking world, which is in desperate need of truth. In addition, each time we give in to lying it spirals down, infecting others in more ways than we can imagine. That's how the devil works: infecting us and those around us through deception.

Satan is seeking to destroy the Christian's testimony, knowing people in the workplace are looking to us to set the standard for ethics, morality, and workplace behavior. When they hear us telling "half-truths" or "white lies," they find it easier to justify their own immorality because of the mediocrity they see in our life.

How much better it would have been for me to take a stand for truth and say, "If it's for me, tell them I'm on my way to a meeting and I'll call them back," or "Whoever it is, I'll need to call them back." That way I'm speaking truth, honoring God's Word, modeling a lifestyle of Christ, and living a moral life in the workplace.

When our colleagues see us live out truth in the workplace, God will be glorified. This is how we live victoriously in the workplace—through day-to-day decisions that put our faith in action and defeat the enemy's lies and deception.

• • •

Personal Insight

What new truths has God revealed to you? How will you depend on the Holy Spirit so you are not taken captive by the world's hollow and deceptive philosophy? _____

_____

_____

_____

• • •

Spiritual Application

Write out the Scripture verse(s) in this chapter that gave you encouragement for your current work situation? _____

_____

_____

_____

How is God speaking to you through this verse? _____

_____

_____

_____

What workplace actions will you commit to following through on as you strive to walk in truth and dismantle the world's deception? _____

_____

_____

_____

2

Prosperous and Successful

Victory in the Workplace

Do not let this Book of the Law depart from your mouth; meditate on it day and night, so that you may be careful to do everything written in it. Then you will be prosperous and successful.

Joshua 1:8

As Christian women we need to continually pursue God's truth in the workplace. In addition, we must surrender our hearts to his will and serve him through a lifestyle of obedience, as we see in the life of Joshua. In summary, in the first chapter of Joshua, the Israelites are still wandering in the desert, Moses has died, and God has just elevated Joshua to the new leadership position of overseeing two million Israelites. Joshua appears to have been given an impossible responsibility—leading the

Fruit of the Spirit

As we choose to be a Joshua (I mean that in the most feminine way!), we too will win numerous office battles, destroy the walls of immorality, and lead our coworkers (and ourselves) from the captivity of deception to spiritual freedom. But only as our lives are saturated with God's Word and we depend on the Holy Spirit's power will we accomplish his will in the workplace.

Jesus says in John 15:5, "I am the vine; you are the branches. If a man remains in me and I in him, he will bear much fruit; apart from me you can do nothing." How privileged we are to be able to be "fruit bearers" bearing much fruit for Jesus. If you've been to a vineyard, you can appreciate this analogy. However, most of us haven't, so let me share with you what my girlfriend Chris shared with me. She said in her straightforward way, "God wants me to tell you that the best fruit is the one that stays closest to the vine." Well, even though I'm a city girl, I knew exactly what she meant and thought, "Yes, that's it, my life will be most fruitful when I stay close to Jesus."

Just like fruit, the closer we stay to the vine, the sweeter our spirits will be, in and out of the workplace. Our job, unlike the job of the farmer who has to plant, gather, and prune his crop in order to reap much fruit, is easy because all we have to do is remain close to the vine.

No amount of hard work or willpower will change the fact that apart from God we will be unfruitful. Instead of harvesting the fruit of the Spirit, which draws others to Christ, our coworkers will see dead fruit, demonstrated by a lifestyle of bitterness, worry, chaos, discontentment, callousness, condemnation, impatience, and inconsistency. When I eat fruit, I want it to look succulent, to be pleasing to my eye, and definitely to be sweet tasting. As Christians in the workplace, the best way to draw others to Christ is to be attractive "fruit bearers."

John 15:8 says, "This is to my Father's glory that you bear much fruit, showing yourselves to be my disciples." As God is glorified by our fruit-bearing, five truths will prevail in our life. First, we will find that being fruitful requires remaining at Jesus' feet. Second, our character will be strengthened and purified to reflect Jesus' character. Third, the light of Jesus that is in us will shine forth in the workplace, exposing darkness and its deception. Fourth, we will, by remaining in Jesus, be an extension of love to our coworkers. And fifth, we will be recipients of God's protection.

With that in mind, let me garnish your plate with a little fruit!

Remaining at Jesus' Feet

The spiritual fruit that comes to mind when I think of being at Jesus' feet is *faithfulness*. In order to remain faithful to what God has called us to do in the workplace, we must consistently walk in humility, knowing that everything we need to be victorious lies at the feet of Jesus. Here in his presence we are strengthened and equipped to do all that God has commissioned us to do in the workplace.

Psalm 31:23 tells us that God preserves the faithful. So when everything at work seems to be falling apart and we are the recipients of undue criticism, let's not become weary or slack but rather be more zealous, knowing that he is faithful to his promise to uphold us.

Mary, sister of Martha and Lazarus, was strengthened at Jesus' feet. On two specific occasions recorded in the Bible, Mary remained at Jesus' feet. On the first occasion Mary welcomes Jesus into her home, and instead of being busy running, running, running, like her sister Martha, she gleans truth at Jesus' feet (Luke 10:38–42). The other time we read about Mary and Jesus, she is once again at his feet. This time however, instead of being criticized by her sister, she's being rebuked by a disciple who thought she was being wasteful by pouring expensive perfume over Jesus' body (John 12:1–8). Despite being misunderstood and scolded, Mary was a fruit bearer of much faithfulness, sitting at the feet of Jesus.

As we commit to being a fruit bearer of faithfulness, we can be encouraged by Mary's life and remain steadfast in the midst of criticism because we know it's at Jesus' feet that we will find strength. He is our very source of life. As we remain faithful to him, we will hear, "Well done, good and faithful servant! You have been faithful with a few things; I will put you in charge of many things. Come and share in your master's happiness!" (Matt. 25:23).

Strengthened in Character

Just as faithfulness is needed to remain in Jesus, *patience* and *self-control* are also needed as God transforms our character into his likeness.

When we reflect on the trials we've endured in the workplace, most of us would agree that God was purifying and strengthening our character while working out our situations. God wants the core of who we are to reflect the full essence of who he is, and for this reason he continues to refine self-control and patience in our character.

We will become fruit bearers as God prunes away our selfish desires and hurriedness. As we commit to being fruit bearers of self-control and patience, we will be tested. Most often the test will come when we desire something and God says, "Wait."

As our character is molded into his, we will be given many opportunities to bear the fruit of self-control and patience—but these opportunities require us to be active participants. We are to be *doers* of God's Word, not just hearers. First Peter 1:13 tells us, "Therefore, prepare your minds for action; be self-controlled; set your hope fully on the grace to be given you when Jesus Christ is revealed."

Light in Darkness

Ephesians 5:8–10 says, "For you were once darkness, but now you are light in the Lord. Live as children of light (for the fruit of the light consists in all goodness, righteousness and truth) and find out what pleases the Lord."

What pleases the Lord is seeing us become fruit bearers of much *goodness* and *love*. Part of being in the light of the Lord requires pursuing love and goodness in the workplace. The goodness we show and the love we extend will be the true indicators of our hearts and will do more for God's moral truth in the workplace than any legislation or code of conduct. Being a fruit bearer for Jesus requires going beyond not doing wrong to doing what we know we ought to do, as was the case with my friend Arlene.

Arlene has been an emergency room nurse for over fourteen years. She's seen just about everything and could easily become hardened by the blood and gore or the needs of her patients, but she hasn't. One day she shared with me the grievous tragedy of a prisoner who was rushed to the emergency room. This prisoner had attempted suicide but failed.

As she tried to find out what had happened and to comfort this patient, the prison guards jeered him, laughed at him, and sarcastically mocked him by saying, "His girlfriend broke up with him." Now Arlene, who is a Christian, could have turned a hard heart to the prisoner, thought "Serves him right," and treated him with disdain. Instead she was an extension of God's goodness and love by speaking kindly to the prisoner, reassuring him that he would be okay. She took care of him just as Jesus cares for us and most likely ministered to this man's soul.

Arlene may never know how that seed of love and goodness will manifest itself in this prisoner's life, but we can be sure of one thing: She was a fruit bearer of much goodness and love. God's Word tells us that whatever we have done for the least of them, we have done for Jesus (Matt. 25:40). This prisoner was one of the least of them. Did Arlene let the light of Jesus shine in a place of darkness? You bet she did, and because of that, God was glorified.

Loving Our Neighbors

Even the world would agree that it's easy to love the lovely, the beautiful, and the kind. But being a fruit bearer requires going beyond loving the lovely to demonstrating the fruit of *kindness* and *gentleness* to the unkind, the unlovely, and the unlikable. In 1 Thessalonians 2:7, Paul gives the church an analogy of true gentleness and kindness in action: a mother caring for her little children.

As a mom, I've spent numerous hours caring for my little ones. I've sacrificed my time, energy, and personal needs to care for their daily needs. So when I read this passage, I know the apostle Paul is requiring us to bear much fruit. This is the fruit God wants us, as Christian women, to bear as we kindly and gently extend ourselves to our coworkers. Only as we become fruit bearers of kindness and gentleness will others see Christ in us.

We can be fruit bearers as we greet the cleaning lady with a warm, kindhearted "hello" or speak a gentle and uplifting word to the coworker who rubs us the wrong way. Or we could even be kind to the colleague who's been undermining our work and attempting to destroy our reputation. Being a "fruit bearer" of kindness and gentleness requires going beyond the expected and showing Jesus through our attitudes and actions.

My friend Noelene did just this and became a fruit bearer for the delivery man dropping a package off at her store. He had been coming into her bookstore frequently for a while and on occasion would unload his heart to her. After listening to him on several occasions, she offered to pray with him and shared the Good News of Jesus' love. Unorthodox, maybe! But as she trusted God she became a fruit bearer to an unlikely neighbor.

Then there's my friend Lisa, who occasionally teaches constitutional law to undergraduate students. One day a student approached her to discuss the family and workload problems that were having an adverse effect on his grades. As she assessed the situation as only an attorney can, she instantly became a fruit bearer with her response. In the midst of her hectic schedule, she stopped to listen and then asked if she could pray with him. Once again a fruit bearer was bringing much glory to God.

Prayer is not the only way to be a fruit bearer of kindness and gentleness. Most often it will only require that we stop in the midst of our busy work schedule to offer a kind word to the unlikely recipient or demonstrate gentleness in our behavior to the unlovely.

God's Protection

Jesus tells us in John 14:27, "Peace I leave with you; my peace I give you. I do not give to you as the world gives. Do not let your hearts be troubled and do not be afraid." Many

not be able to discern truth from darkness, nor will we be able to see the relevance of applying God's Word to our lives.

Most of us know God's Word but still feel defeated when it comes to application. Have you ever had a good devotional time and then two or three hours later forgotten what your devotional was about? This is where most of us get stuck! Just as we need learning "tools" to help us apply new skills in the workplace, we need "tools" for learning God's Word.

The "tools" I have are a Bible concordance, Bible with four parallel translations, a study Bible, three different types of dictionaries (Hebrew and Greek, English, and Bible dictionary), my journal, and a notebook. In addition, I use various commentaries and computer programs with Bible reference materials.

Depending on your time constraints or the Bible passage you are studying, you may use only one or two of these reference materials. Sometimes I only have time for reading a verse and journaling. For example, I may address three life application questions for Psalm 18:1, "I love you, O LORD, my strength." I may write:

1. What does this passage say about God? *God is my strength!*

2. How does God's truth affect my life? *When I feel like I can't go on, he is my strength.*

3. How can I apply this truth to my life? *I love you, Lord, and will demonstrate that love to you by placing my day in your hands, knowing that you are my strength. When something unexpected happens today, I will not be discouraged or overwhelmed, because you are my strength. Thank you, Lord!*

That night I may go back to this same verse and look up the word *strength* in my Hebrew and Greek dictionary, meditating further on what it means. Or I may go to the Bible concordance and look up other passages that use the word *strength*.

As we learn God's Word and meditate on it, we become more able to extract life-changing truths for ourselves and apply them to our lives, which leads us to the next principle.

Now we come to the third and most challenging principle: *following!* Jesus says in Luke 11:28, "Blessed rather are those who hear the word of God and obey it." It's useless to journal or write down what we are going to do if we don't follow through. If we want to experience victory in any part of our lives, we must *do!* Doing requires being a fruit bearer of faithfulness, patience, and self-control. Faithfulness in action requires doing even when we don't feel like it. Patience in action means doing even when we don't see the immediate benefit. And self-control in action requires doing in order to obey.

Following God's Word day to day in the workplace is hard. That's why God gave us the Holy Spirit to help us and enable us. We can never do all God has called us to do without the Holy Spirit. That's why Galatians 5:22 says "the fruit of the Spirit," not "the fruit of the *self*" is love, joy, peace, patience, kindness, goodness, faithfulness, gentleness, and self-control. When everything in us says, "The call is too great; the burden is too heavy," we must remember to rely on the Spirit in us.

Although the weight of being a Christian woman in the workplace seems overwhelming at times, God knows how much we can bear and is waiting for us to give him all our burdens. When we are tempted to quit or compromise God's truth in the workplace, let's remember that it's not our own strength but the power of the Holy Spirit that allows us to live in truth (John 16:13). In him we are able to hear, learn, and follow!

Work and Worship

As we follow the principles of hearing, learning, and following, we will begin to see the workplace as another avenue to glorify God. Work will no longer just be a place to achieve more or earn a living but a place of worship. Consider the difference this perspective makes:

> There is a story that when the famed English architect, Sir Christopher Wren, was directing the building of St. Paul's Cathedral in London, some of the workers were interviewed by a journalist who asked them, "What are you doing here?" The first said, "I'm cutting stone for three shillings a day." The second replied, "I'm putting ten hours a day on this job." The third replied, "I'm helping Sir Christopher Wren build the greatest cathedral in Great Britain for the glory of God."[1]

As we begin living out God's truth in the workplace through the power of the Holy Spirit in us, we will experience victory in areas we've long given up on. Our attitudes, lifestyles, and values will change drastically, and others will be drawn to Christ. We will know what it means to be prosperous and successful according to God's Word.

God has commissioned and equipped each of us to spread the Good News of the gospel, so wherever he places us as part of our occupation is his holy territory. Just as Joshua ordered his officers to "take possession of the land the LORD your God is giving you for your own" (Josh. 1:11), I hear him echoing those same words to us as Christian women in the workplace. As a "Joshua wannabe" I say, "Ladies, let's take the land, feed his sheep, bring light into darkness, give hope to the hopeless! Make this place of work a place of holy territory for Jesus' sake!"

• • •

Personal Insight

What new truths has God revealed to you? How has God's promise of success and prosperity changed your way of thinking? _____

_____

_____

_____

• • •

Spiritual Application

Write out the Scripture verse(s) in this chapter that gave you encouragement for your current work situation. ____ ____

_____

_____

_____

How is God speaking to you through this verse? _____

_____

_____

_____

What workplace actions will you commit to as you become a fruit bearer for Jesus Christ? _____

_____

_____

_____

3

A Woman of Noble Character

Who You Are at Work

And now, my daughter, don't be afraid. I will do for you all
you ask. All my fellow townsmen know that you are a woman
of noble character.

Ruth 3:11

D o you know someone personally you would call *a
woman of noble character?* Better yet, would anyone
say this about you? To be honest, I can hardly begin
to call myself "a woman of noble character," let alone profess
to have lived a lifestyle in the workplace that would qualify
me for this coveted title.

But as a woman of noble character in the making—and let
me emphasize *in the making*—I share with you spiritual truths
and personal experiences on how we all can govern our lives

to reflect God, enabling us to become that woman of noble character.

As I draw truths and examples from the Book of Ruth, I pray you will be blessed by her life as a Christian working woman. So often we admire Ruth, whose name means "friend," for her loyal commitment to her mother-in-law Naomi or embrace the romantic love story between her and Boaz. We would do a grave injustice to Ruth if her story ended there, for she is a role model for today's working woman. She defies the world's definition of success and moves into a higher realm—victory in the workplace!

As Ruth takes us on her journey, let us learn from her experiences as an unemployed, destitute Moabite widow who becomes the great-grandmother of King David, an ancestor to Jesus. I pray we are encouraged and richly blessed through her story, a story from one working woman to another.

Being a woman of noble character like Ruth has to do with our "esteem," or value. Our true esteem is how God views us—his high regard for us over our own estimation of who we are. The important thing is not our "self-esteem," how we feel about ourselves, but our true esteem, the way God feels about us.

We often try to tie our esteem to our careers or current circumstances. Think about how you describe yourself. Does your career take up most of the conversation? Do you find yourself giving your work credentials more significance than being the fun-loving or tenderhearted woman you are?

I'm guilty on both accounts. In the past I placed so much of my self-worth and value in my job titles, experiences, and various positions that over a period of time my true identity was swallowed up by what I did, who I worked for, and what part of town I worked in. As hard as it is for me to admit now,

I allowed the world's distorted concept of identity and value to suffocate God's truth of who I am as a Christian woman.

Most of us base our esteem in ourselves instead of in the Lord, unlike Ruth, who is a prime example of a woman esteemed in the Lord. Instead of focusing on who she was as an unemployed widow from a foreign land, she wrapped her identity in God. She boldly declares, "Your people will be my people and your God my God" (Ruth 1:16). As she embraces God for herself, she accepts everything that comes from this truth, including being esteemed in him. She does not let her ethnic background, personal status, national origin, or even religious affiliation get in the way of taking on her true identity in the Lord.

Ruth easily could have decided to cleave to the familiar and do what was expected of her. Instead, she makes the commitment to place her identity and value in God, valuing his great and powerful image over her own frailties and insecurities.

Valuing God's Image

When the esteem of our core being is not based in our relationship with God, it doesn't matter what title, professional status, or salary we have, we'll always feel a void in our lives. Our esteem is in God alone. But coming to this place requires radically changing our identity and value from self to God. We must move beyond the world's concept of "self-esteem" and stand on four central Scriptural truths that will give us a new identity in "God-esteem."

The first truth is what God's Word says about the essence of who we are. Genesis 1:27 says, "God created man in his own image." Let's pause right here and grasp the truth of what this Scripture means. We can have no greater value or significance than being created in God's image. Since God thought enough of us to create us in his image, I think the least we can do is embrace the value that comes from being created in the Almighty's image.

We must not only take hold of this awesome truth but etch it on our hearts. Failure to take hold of this truth will keep us bound in self, status, and everything that is contrary to God's Word. We are a reflection of God, created in his image. This must be the first foundational truth for self-image.

The second truth is seen in Psalm 139:13–14: "For you created my inmost being; you knit me together in my mother's womb. I praise you because I am fearfully and wonderfully made; your works are wonderful, I know that full well." When was the last time you praised God for creating you just the way you are, fearfully and wonderfully made? If you can't think of a recent time you praised him for his creation, then do so right now! We must be willing to change our way of thinking about our self, our value, and our esteem. It's only when we begin taking God at his Word, as demonstrated through our attitude and actions, that we'll experience this truth in our life.

Most of us don't experience the truth that we are fearfully and wonderfully made because we keep believing the enemy, his lies, and our self-doubt. This type of thinking is contrary to God's Word and causes us to focus on and value what self can and cannot do instead of what God has done and will do.

The next time you start driving down that road of being esteemed in self instead of being esteemed in God, mentally pull over and begin praising him for his truth that you are fearfully and wonderfully made by the Creator himself.

I believe this is what Ruth must have done. Just imagine: To the world she seemed to have everything stacked against her. How could she have any esteem left? After all, she came from a despised lineage as a Moabite, and she was widowed, a foreigner, and unemployed. Why don't we see an attitude of despair? I believe it's because her value was rooted in the Lord.

The third truth we must embrace is that as Christian women we can graciously accept the great privileges that come from having a Father who reigns in heaven and earth. Romans 8:16 says, "The Spirit himself testifies with our spirit that we are God's children." First John 3:1 says, "How great is the love the Father has lavished on us, that we should be called children of God!" What a great privilege it is to be heirs with God and coheirs with his Son.

Ruth accepted the privileges that come from being a child of God, daughter of the King! When we place our trust in God and accept Jesus as Lord and Savior of our lives, we are in essence letting him know that we want the privileges that come with this trust. Just as Ruth trusted God, her Father, to meet all her needs, we can trust him to meet our spiritual, emotional, and physical needs, in and out of the workplace.

The fourth truth we must receive is the freedom that comes from being esteemed in the Lord. Great liberty comes from not having our esteem tied to our job titles, our nationality, our gender, or the status quo. This liberty lays the groundwork for focusing on what is really important: becoming a woman of noble character, which has nothing to do with what we do but comes from who we are in Christ. Galatians 2:20 says, "I have been crucified with Christ and I no longer live, but Christ lives in me. The life I live in the body, I live by faith in the Son of God." The old, valueless self that taunted us is now replaced with the life of Christ—who is all-powerful, righteous, and of immeasurable value.

If Ruth had not been esteemed in the Lord, he would not have been able to work through her, because she would have been placing undue importance on her circumstances and what she could or could not "bring to the table." But instead we see a life of value that unfolds beautifully because of her acceptance of God in her life. As we trust God for our value and esteem, he is able to give us a new identity, just as he gave Ruth her new identity so she could experience him as her true God.

Dressing Appropriately

"Wash and perfume yourself, and put on your best clothes" (Ruth 3:3). This excellent advice for today's Christian woman was first spoken by Naomi to Ruth.

Depending on who you ask, you may hear many different definitions of dressing for success. Therefore my premise for dress will be what 1 Corinthians 6:19–20 says: "Do you not know that your body is a temple of the Holy Spirit, who is in you, whom you have received from God? You are not your own; you were bought at a price. Therefore honor God with your body." From this passage we know our dress can bring either honor or dishonor to God.

As Christian women, how we dress in the workplace speaks volumes on how we value God's temple. Our bodies are a dwelling place for the Holy Spirit. However, this does not mean that we need to cover ourselves in black sackcloth to honor God. Personally, I love looking my absolute best. God is the creator of beauty, so let's not buy into the misconception that honoring God means giving up our own sense of style, fashion, or beauty. The key is honoring God.

I remember a time not so long ago when my style of dressing had nothing to do with honoring God and everything to do with trends, style, and self. Always being rather conservative and conscientious, I never wore anything outlandish, but

I don't recall ever giving thought to honoring God through my outward appearance.

For instance, for a time I sported a number of those really short skirt suits—three or four inches above the knee—in my attempt to keep up with fashion. The fact is, some professionals would not have considered what I wore to be inappropriate. However, I know now I was not honoring God because I always felt that too much attention was being directed to my body. To begin with, I never felt comfortable sitting in those short skirts; they always inched up a notch or two when I sat down, exposing even more of my legs. And if I had a meeting scheduled for the day, I would strategically sit behind my office desk or place a clipboard, papers, or something else over my lap. This was my attempt at being modest.

For the sake of consistency, let me reiterate that appropriate dress is not about the length of your skirt but about the depths of your heart. If we are dressing for the approval of others or placing self-serving interests above a desire to please God, as I was, then we are not honoring God.

Dressing should be another outward sign of our love for God. When we dress to honor God, our inner and outer beauty blossoms like a beautiful orchid. As we determine what is or is not appropriate dress for a woman of noble character, we need to assess our motives and what's in our heart.

Each of us has to come to a point of accountability before God and ask some heartfelt questions: Does what I'm wearing reflect my relationship with God? Does my heavenly Father feel honored or shamed by this outfit? Does this outfit increase or diminish my credibility as a professional?

God has called each of us to be a woman of noble character. So as we seek to bring glory to God through our sense of style and fashion, we should consider purity, comfort, professionalism, and femininity. I have not written them in order of importance, because I believe all of these components are equally important parts of the whole.

I address purity because it speaks to the heart of who we are as Christian women. If we dress to draw undue attention to ourselves or even to please others, I believe we need to consider our motives and ask ourselves, "Is my heart pure? Am I seeking God with all my heart (Psalm 119:9–10)?"

Comfort is essential for today's career woman. We have so many roles to play and tasks to oversee that being uncomfortable for any length of time is unnecessary. If what we are wearing is too tight, it will be both uncomfortable and unflattering. And just as something looks unflattering when worn too tightly, the same can be true when something is worn too loosely.

Have you ever seen someone wearing a blouse that's a size too big so that when she bends over her undergarments are exposed? Well, it's just as inappropriate to have undergarments show as it is to see undergarments pressed tightly under something. In both situations the woman looks unprofessional, uncomfortable, and very inappropriately dressed.

No matter what kind of fashion statement you make, make sure you look like the professional and Christian career woman you are. The way you dress should bring increased credibility to you and your position. Let's consider the woman who presents a crisp, clean, professional look. Most likely when others see her they not only see professionalism but also associate her attire with what she does and how well she does it. Whether that assumption is true or not, it is the natural tendency. Conversely, take the same woman and dress her in a sloppy, uncaring manner. How likely is it that others will attach that same sloppy, uncaring look to how she does her job? People generally connect how someone dresses—whether good, bad, or indifferent—with the quality of work she does.

Lastly, I believe that as Christian women, we need to place a premium on femininity. So often in today's society, femininity is looked upon in a negative sense. As women we have bought into the idea that in order to be successful in the workplace, we need to dress like men and take on masculine attributes, down to wearing a blue suit and white blouse. Not only is that look unnecessary, but it denies us the inherent right to be as God created us—feminine beings. As we strive to honor God with our dress, let's not be afraid to let our inner and outer beauty come through. After all, a woman of noble character is unique in character and in dress.

Seeking Wisdom, Demonstrating Integrity

A woman of noble character cares about her outward appearance, and she's even more concerned about her character. In the opening pages of Ruth we see godly character traits unfold in her life. First she seeks wisdom from her mother-in-law when deciding to glean in Boaz's field. Next we see a woman of integrity as she presents herself honestly, with no pretenses, to those around her.

As we find ourselves immersed in the daily challenges of the workplace, we will undoubtedly be placed in situations in which we'll need to seek wisdom as well as demonstrate integrity. Failure to do so can mean the difference between failing or succeeding.

Over the course of my career, I've sought God's wisdom countless times before, during, and after a decision. At other times I was afraid to go to God for fear of where he would lead me. And then again, sometimes I was in that all too familiar but dreaded situation called "between a rock and a hard place," where it's easiest to avoid making a decision because you know no matter what you do, you are sunk!

But it's in the midst of these difficult and challenging times we most need to seek godly wisdom. James 3:17 says, "But the wisdom that comes from heaven is first of all pure; then peace-loving, considerate, submissive, full of mercy and good fruit, impartial and sincere."

I recall a specific time when disciplining an employee could have resulted in one of three possible scenarios: termination for the employee, facing a wrongful termination suit, or extending the employee's probation period, which would have meant subjecting his coworkers to another bout of hostile treatment. All possible outcomes had my stomach in knots.

In such dire situations, our best recourse is to go to God in prayer, meditate on his Word, and trust him for wisdom. In the Book of James we are told, "If any of you lacks wisdom, he should ask God, who gives generously to all without finding fault, and it will be given to him" (James 1:5).

How freeing and exciting it is to know that wisdom is ours for the asking. And regardless of the outcome, we can have peace because we know that we sought God in faith for direction, discernment, and a wise decision. Lanson Ross, author of *Total Life Prosperity,* sums up the freedom that comes from faith-based decisions this way: "Faith is the key word in the decision-making process. None of us knows when we make a decision exactly how things will turn out."[1]

When I needed to discipline that employee, I did not know the impact of my decision, so I had to walk in faith, trusting God to lead and direct me and then to work everything out for his good. This did not make my situation any less stressful, but it did free me as I trusted God for all aspects of the decision.

This sounds all well and good, you may be thinking, but what if you seek God in prayer, meditate on his Word, and hear nothing, absolutely *nothing?* In this situation I encourage you to do at least one of two things: First, seek the counsel of another Christian, someone who is spiritually mature and discerning, or go to a trusted professional in confidence, someone who understands the dynamics of the situation and doesn't have a vested interest in the outcome.

However, before you seek any kind of outside counsel, make certain that you have not abandoned your decision-making responsibilities and that you are obeying God in this direction. If God is not leading you to outside counsel, then you are no longer walking in faith but in fear and disobedience.

Seeking wisdom requires an obedient heart. Wisdom and obedience go hand in hand. As we seek wisdom we must go to God and trust that he'll provide an answer. In the past, when I earnestly sought God for a decision, I can honestly say now that he wasn't silent but rather answering me in a way I did not expect.

Brian L. Harbour, author of several studies on the New Testament, says, "God's wisdom is measured in a different way from the world's wisdom. We do not have to be in who's who to know what's what. We do not have to be well known in the world to be well knowing. Real wisdom comes from God. It is obtained through a vital relationship with Him, and it will manifest itself in our life in certain ways."[2] Being a vessel means doing whatever God says even when we don't understand what God is doing.

Can you imagine Ruth's life had she not trusted God or sought wise counsel from Naomi? Remember, it was Naomi who advised her to go the threshing floor and lie at the feet of Boaz. Naomi's advice may seem unusual and somewhat suspect, but as the story unfolds we see that her advice is both wise and part of God's divine plan to bless Ruth's life.

This brings us to another point: demonstrating integrity. Ruth displays honesty without assumption when she humbles herself and gleans behind the harvesters. How easy it would have been for her to assert herself and expect to glean in the fields, either in front of the harvesters or in an assumed position beside the servant girls. Instead she chooses integrity and humility over a haughty and selfish spirit.

As Christian working women, we all could learn a lesson about humility in the workplace. I know I can! A couple of years ago, while I was working as a director of human resources, the CEO asked me to get a round of coffee for everyone. Yes, I complied with his request, but I mulled over the situation for weeks on end, thinking, "Who does he think I am? I'm not his servant. He could have asked someone else."

In spite of the fact that I do believe he was exerting his authority and power over me to prove a point, my attitude was wrong as a Christian woman. Had the core of my esteem been rooted in my relationship with the Lord, as we talked about earlier, I would not have been so bothered. I still might not have liked the position he placed me in, but I would not have spent so much time thinking about it or gotten myself so bent out of shape about it.

Through her attitude and strong work ethic, Ruth demonstrates godly character woven in integrity. Even the foreman praises her as he declares, "She went into the field and has worked steadily from morning till now, except for a short rest in the shelter" (Ruth 2:7). Through her strong work ethic, she is able to bring glory to God and receive respect from those in authority over her.

Ruth also demonstrates integrity through a consistent lifestyle aligned with God's Word. When everything is said and done, if our lifestyles in the workplace don't line up with what we say, no one will believe a word we say, no matter how loudly we shout! Coworkers will only hear what we live. Therefore God must be the source of our integrity.

Controlling Emotions

As the meeting came to an end, streams of tears ran down my cheeks. My spirit was broken. I could hardly speak. How dare my boss question my integrity? He could question decisions I made, but question my integrity? That was off limits and more than I could take.

I was tired of standing alone, fighting the good fight. At that moment all I could do was surrender myself to a flood of emotions. Within minutes I was sobbing uncontrollably, standing in a pool of tears.

Have you ever been in a similar situation? Have you run to the ladies' rest room for composure or excused yourself from a meeting in order not to break down in front of others? Well, I've been there, done that!

With the stresses and demands of our working environment, it's a wonder we don't break down in tears more often. Shedding tears over the challenges we face in the workplace is nothing to be ashamed of or point a finger at. As women, we tend to be more vulnerable to emotional releases because we tend to take things to heart. The fact that we are made with emotions is a great blessing from God.

Our emotions are the gateway to compassion. We need compassion to reach out to others as they experience some of these same joys and pains in life. However, as I've learned, if we don't bring our emotions under God's authority and Word, we will be swimming in a pool of tears . . . constantly!

Wouldn't it be great if we could all have Ruth's emotional resolve? She resolved to walk in faith and not in emotions. At the beginning of the Book of Ruth, we are introduced to Orpah and Ruth, who are experiencing similar situations. Both women are grieving the loss of their husband, having to face the harsh realities of being a widow, and knowing their dreams for the future will probably never happen.

In spite of the fact that they have their own individual uniqueness, differences, and emotional backgrounds, these women are a source of comfort for one another. They can relate to what the other is experiencing. In their attempt to find comfort, security, and a new beginning, they both agree to follow Naomi to Bethlehem. However, upon further reading, we see that Orpah changes her mind. She decides to remain in her homeland, which is not necessarily wrong. But I believe her decision was based on emotions. In any case, I find it interesting to note that we don't hear of Orpah again.

Ruth, on the other hand, resolved to trust God and becomes a direct ancestor of Jesus through King David. Does this have anything to do with her resolve and not letting her emotions control her? Well, I can't be sure, but I do know that if she had changed her mind, we probably wouldn't have a Book of Ruth.

Ruth is appealing to me because, unlike me, she is unwavering in her trust of God. Despite the temptation to rethink her situation or to second-guess the wisdom of following her mother-in-law, she stays the course. If you were in her situation, would you change your mind? Ruth stays the course and says, "May the LORD deal with me, be it ever so severely, if anything but death separates you and me" (Ruth 1:17).

Wow, talk about emotional resolve! Ruth doesn't get emotionally sidetracked with how she feels, the weather, or even if she's having a bad hair day. Instead, she is faithful to her commitment. As we become involved in various situations in the workplace, we need this resolve to obey and do what God asks of us.

The enemy wants to use our emotions to get us sidetracked from obeying God and walking in his will. The enemy uses our emotions to keep us second-guessing God's plan for our life and his purpose for us in the workplace. As soon as we let our spiritual guard down, the enemy is right there using our emotions to foster doubt and question our purpose.

As we seek to control our emotions with the Holy Spirit's guidance, we need to stay rooted in God's Word and concentrate on what I call the "FACT" of the matter: Focus, Act, Control, and Think!

First, we need to *focus* on being a vessel for the Lord. This means placing our Christian testimony above our personal gain, desire, or feelings. As we focus on being a vessel for the Lord, not only will he reward us for our obedience, but others will be drawn to him by what they see. Focus on doing what is right in the sight of God, not on how we feel.

Second, *act* instead of react! Oftentimes in the workplace we react like a loose cannon—firing out the first thing that comes to mind. We put little thought into what we say, because we react from raw emotions instead of acting in accordance with God's Word or leading. Once a difficult situation arises, discipline yourself to gather your thoughts first, either by waiting a minute before responding or by giving yourself a couple of hours to evaluate your decision. If this is not possible, postpone your decision or response until the next day, after you've had time to sleep on it.

Third, *control* your feelings by remaining neutral. This is slightly different from the above because it deals with preventing yourself from feeling personally attacked. When we don't control our feelings, we surrender them to others, and this is what causes an emotional release. Don't let the enemy or others in the workplace have that kind of power over you. Instead, opt to control the situation by controlling your emotions and seeing the situation from the other point of view. This is not to say that we have to bottle up our feelings, but as much as possible vent those feelings to a safe confidante or at a later time when you are removed from the situation. When expressing yourself in times of duress, stay away from "emotionally charged" words that incite personal reactions and state the facts as much as possible. Remember Detective Friday from *Dragnet*? "Just the facts, ma'am, just the facts!"

And lastly, *think!* Think about any extenuating circumstances. Think about the truth as everyone being affected in the situation sees it. Think about your role in the situation. Ask yourself, "Was there anything I could have done to prevent that situation from occurring?" "What is God trying to teach me through this situation?" "What character issue is God working on in my life?" and finally, "Were exaggerations made to strengthen my point or heighten my feelings?"

In the most trying situations, we can always learn something. The primary reason for controlling your emotions is that you know God is on your side (Psalm 56:9). The enemy wants to use our emotions to destroy us, but Isaiah 41:13 reassures us: "For I am the LORD, your God, who takes hold of your right hand and says to you, Do not fear; I will help you."

As we aspire to become women of noble character, we can thank God for giving us Ruth, the quintessential woman experiencing victory in the workplace. Ruth lived for God, ministered to others, and was used in her lowly position as a vessel of change to bring forth the King of Kings! We can consider

Ruth a true mentor as we seek to one day be known as "a woman of noble character."

• • •

Personal Insight

What two character traits do you feel are most essential to being a woman of noble character and why? _____

_____

_____

_____

• • •

Spiritual Application

Write out the Scripture verse(s) in this chapter that gave you encouragement for your current work situation. _____

_____

_____

_____

How is God speaking to you through this verse? _____

_____

_____

_____

What workplace actions will you commit to as you strive to be a woman of noble character? _____

_____

_____

_____

4

Full of Grace, Seasoned with Salt

Communication in the Workplace

Let your conversation be always full of grace, seasoned with salt, so that you may know how to answer everyone.

Colossians 4:6

A s a young college student I was intrigued with human communication—so much so that I majored in psychology and communications. With the lethal weapons of a communications degree in one pocket and a psychology degree in the other, I set out to astound the world with my "vast knowledge."

Two decades and scores of workshops later, human communication still mystifies me. Like many of you, I've mastered the basic elements of communication yet desire to communicate beyond the surface level. For this to happen, however, we must first grasp that communication in its true essence is not an art form but a heart issue: "For out of the overflow of the heart the mouth speaks" (Matt. 12:34).

At the heart of communication are prayer, truth, wisdom, grace, and love, all of which are addressed in this chapter. Communicating beyond the basics requires studying the most exhaustive and comprehensive communications manual on the market: the Bible. Our communications professor, if I may call him this, will be the apostle Paul. He comes highly recommended and has an illustrious resume. Just to give you a glimpse of his qualifications, let me say that he is heralded as one of history's most dynamic leaders, a phenomenal orator, a prolific writer of numerous books, and, most importantly, a servant-worker for Jesus Christ.

The Heart of Communication

Americans are granted certain inherent rights, including "freedom of speech." For the most part we can say whatever we want, whenever we want, to whomever we want and be protected under the First Amendment.

However, as Christians our freedom is not freedom of speech but freedom from sin. We are never to use our freedom to cover up for evil (1 Peter 2:16) or our communication to say whatever we feel like. James 3:6 tells us that an untamed tongue can corrupt the whole person. Therefore, when we exercise the freedom of speech, we should use it to communicate the message of the gospel of Christ's love, as Paul writes:

> Devote yourself to prayer, being watchful and thankful. And pray for us, too, that God may open a door for our message, so that we may proclaim the mystery of Christ, for which I

am in chains. Pray that I may proclaim it clearly, as I should. Be wise in the way you act toward outsiders; make the most of every opportunity. Let your conversation be always full of grace, seasoned with salt, so that you may know how to answer everyone.

Colossians 4:2–6

Although various communication theories and freedoms are prevalent in our workplaces, Paul lays a very different foundation for communicating heart to heart. It's only in Christ that we are able to move beyond the *art* of communication to the *heart* of communication and become relevant and effective communicators. Regardless of how eloquent your speech or fine your prose, hurting people want to see the relevance of the Good News in their day-to-day lives. Jesus knew this! He fully understood the importance of being an effective and relevant communicator and practiced it as he presented parables, stories, and thought-provoking questions in his teachings. He always communicated heart to heart, connecting with people where they were. The apostle Paul understood this, and we must also if we are to be effective and relevant communicators of the gospel.

The only way to accomplish this is through the Holy Spirit enabling us. If we rely on ourselves, we will experience communication burnout, fall back into using only the art of communication, become burdensome, and ultimately have little to no powerful impact on those around us through our words.

However, when we rely wholly on God's Word and the Holy Spirit's power, we have the opportunity to touch our everyday work environment as we communicate heart to heart. Our conversations become extensions of Christ that can heal relationships, build bridges, and develop meaningful work relationships, ultimately drawing others to him. Let's look at how the five principles of "communication of the heart" Paul gives us can help us transform our workplaces for God's glory.

Communicating in the Workplace: The Principle of Prayer

Paul begins his instructions to Christians on how to be effective and relevant communicators with "Devote yourself to prayer" (v. 2). Prayer is our first principle of communication of the heart. Oswald Chambers wrote, "If we think of prayer as the breath in our lungs and the blood from our hearts, we think rightly. Prayer is not an exercise, it is the life."[1] For Christians, prayer should be like breathing—we cannot exist apart from it. We are given no greater privilege than prayer, hear no greater voice than God, and experience no greater intimacy than communing with Jesus Christ.

God desires for us to know him and gives us direct access through his Son (John 14:6). Prayer is the best wireless communication plan, bar none! What other communication device provides instant access, no waiting, no numbers, and unlimited service?

To become effective and relevant communicators both in and out of the workplace, we must be devoted to prayer, as Paul instructs us. Prayer is the key that unlocks the door to communicating heart to heart with a distraught employee, a depressed coworker, or a friend struggling to make peace in the workplace.

I can recall a time when prayer opened the door to finding peace and contentment for a friend in the workplace. My friend Pat has worked in almost every area of human resources and office administration for at least fifteen years. When it comes to meeting the demanding challenges of the fast-paced work environment, she tackles them head-on. However, in

70

one particular conversation, as she questioned what spiritual impact she was having on her coworkers, I could tell she was stressed from her heavy workload. She was sapped of energy and tired of being the "go-getter." So in the midst of our conversation, we stopped and prayed. We asked God for wisdom, a renewed heart for work ministry, and emotional refreshment to do his will, and then we resumed our conversation.

About two weeks passed until our next conversation, but this time she couldn't stop talking about answered prayers, a coworker she was ministering to, and God's revealed truth—all because of prayer. Her most exciting news had to do with arriving to work fifteen minutes early to pray for her coworkers while still sitting in the parking lot. She could hardly contain her excitement, nor could I.

As she talked about God's faithfulness, we both clearly saw that God had exceeded our prayer requests and was using Pat's words to transform her and the working environment. She even began greeting her coworkers on Mondays with "Thank God it's Monday!" The communication principle of prayer changed her conversation, opened doors for the gospel, and blessed me with a word of encouragement for my own ministry. When we devote time to communicating with God in prayer, he strengthens us, refreshes us, and places truth in our hearts so we can communicate as effective and relevant Christians.

This all sounds great, but how or when do we have time to pray during our already busy workday? Well, let me answer a question with a question: During your workday are you ever simultaneously talking on the phone, jotting down notes, downloading a file, giving your daily calendar the once-over, and mentally listing everything that needs your attention once you get home? I thought so!

If we can tackle all this without batting an eye, we can also devote time to prayer smack in the middle of accomplishing our other responsibilities. The same "mode" we use to jump-start our multi-task thinking for surviving the workplace can work with this aspect of communication.

Over the next week begin consciously thinking of all the "downtime" you have in your day. Before you laugh and ask, "What downtime?" let me point out a few possibilities: waiting for a client to arrive, waiting for a meeting to start or end, when you are on hold, riding in the elevator, standing in line for lunch, or daydreaming while waiting for that very chatty person to come up for air (yes, this counts).

Any time you allow your mind to wander or shift into neutral is potential downtime. Personally, I try to use these times as opportunities for prayer. Then there is the "cooling-off" time I need every now and again. We've all been there: Someone says or does something that ruffles our feathers. Instead of mentally counting to ten, as the communication gurus tell us to do, we can start praying over our response. God gives each of us twenty-four hours every day, and within this time he provides endless opportunities to communicate with him.

Let's consider a couple of the above downtime situations: being placed on hold and waiting for a meeting to start. When on hold you can pray for the person on the other end of the telephone line, seek the right words to speak, or even thank God for this precious nugget of free time to rest your mind. We all have too many meetings to attend. Nonetheless, during these times you could pray for the person sitting next to you and give him or her an encouraging word. That encouraging word may be as simple as "Hi!" For all you know, no one has spoken to this person all day. No matter how we look at it, communicating with God has unlimited blessings and benefits. We never know how he will use our words to plant a seed of hope in someone's life.

Once we internalize the power and intimacy of prayer, we'll begin to see the daily opportunities God presents us with as a privilege. We will no longer be placed on hold or wait for a meeting to begin without at least thinking about praying. This is praying without ceasing in everyday life.

Communicating Person to Person: The Principle of Truth

Francis Frangipane says, "To ascend toward God is to walk into a furnace of truth where falsehood is extracted from our souls. To abide in the holy place we must dwell in honesty, even when a lie might seem to save us. Truth is knowing God's heart as it was revealed in Christ."[2] In Zechariah 8:16 God instructs us to speak the truth to one another. Truth, our second principle for communication of the heart, is what separates Christians from the world.

Paul challenges believers to go beyond our comfort level so we can proclaim the truth. Webster's dictionary defines *proclaim* as "to announce publicly or officially; to declare (war, peace); to reveal as."[3] When we are proclaiming God's truth, we must not be ashamed to proclaim war against the enemy's lies, even if keeping quiet or misrepresenting the whole truth seems like the "best" solution.

During my initial years in management, I had an employee who felt that lying was her "best" solution. She did not lie about just one thing but many. Her words were stirring up havoc in the office. After a time of contemplation, counsel, and prayer, I confronted her in the privacy of my office and talked about the ensuing consequences. Unfortunately she continued to lie. As much as I wanted to understand and make excuses for her, we needed a trustworthy employee. Eventually she was let go.

someone outside the Christian culture with a Sunday morning "Praise God!" followed by a warm "I love you" hug and a departing word of "Have a blessed week!" and see what kind of response you get. Wise communication with "outsiders" will be done in a way they can understand and that will not turn them away.

For a number of years I worked with a manager who considered himself to be a considerate and accepting person who valued differences and diversity. In the course of our working relationship, we talked about race relations and male-female gender issues within the workplace. On one occasion a colleague invited some coworkers to an after work social. I graciously accepted and invited a longtime friend to join me. As my friend and I entered the foyer, this manager greeted us with a loud and boisterous, "Give me five!" Stunned beyond belief and embarrassed (but more for him than for ourselves), we attempted to make light of the situation and proceeded into the main room—but not until after a one-minute conversation about why we weren't going to "give him five."

Not only did this man fail to use wisdom in relation to our cultural and ethnic differences, but he also succeeded in isolating me from future heart-to-heart conversations with him. Proverbs 12:18 says, "Reckless words pierce like a sword, but the tongue of the wise brings healing." Just as his words pierced my heart and caused unnecessary distance, we separate ourselves from others when we profess the love of Christ with our mouths but behave in a contradictory manner.

When we are not wise and careful with our words and actions, we isolate others. Neglecting Paul's instruction often makes those without Christ feel inferior, isolated, or, worse yet, that Christianity is reproachable and of little value.

Christians in the workplace must always look at diversity as an opportunity to share the Good News of Jesus Christ with others. My sister-in-love (as I affectionately refer to her) Tiffany gave me a birthday card that read, "O Lord, what a variety you have made! And in wisdom you have made them all. The earth is full of your riches" (Ps. 104:24). I kept the card to remind myself of God's beauty in each of us, including both those inside the Christian culture and those outside.

As we strive to become effective and relevant communicators, we must strive to communicate heart to heart and lay aside the natural tendencies to alienate others based on cultural, religious, or physical differences. If we believe the gospel to be truth, then God doesn't need us to defend his Word—he just wants us to speak his words.

A person who communicates under the umbrella of wisdom recognizes the splendor of God's diverse creation and does not use these differences to measure value or worth. All of us struggle to communicate outside of our comfort zones, but this is the place at which we elevate the love of Christ.

Lastly, a person walking in wisdom seeks to be an inclusive communicator. Since Paul instructs us on how to act toward outsiders, we must assume that he anticipates our interaction with them. As we use wisdom to communicate across cultures in the workplace, we must not become isolationist or homogenous in our thinking or communication.

As we become relevant and excellent communicators, we must reach beyond our natural Christian cultural tendencies and "make the most of every opportunity" to share the gospel of Christ with everyone. The gospel of Jesus Christ is not just for some but for everyone. The power of godly wisdom transcends cultural, religious, and personal boundaries.

Communicating to Encourage:
The Principle of Grace

When asked to define grace, most Christians respond, "Undeserved favor from God," and others use words like "gentleness," "kindness," "love," or "a gift." *Strong's Hebrew and Greek Dictionary* defines grace as "especially the divine influence upon the heart, and its reflection of the life."[4] This definition most captures my understanding of the word grace; however, I am reticent to harness such a magnificent and magnanimous word with this or any other definition. The human mind is so finite that it would be foolish to think we could ever fully grasp the fullness of such a God-given gift. After all, no gift from God can be completely understood in our mind.

We must conclude that grace, our fourth communication principle, is vitally important to becoming effective and relevant communicators of the gospel. When Paul writes, "Let your conversation be always full of grace, seasoned with salt" (Col. 4:6), he unapologetically raises the communication standard for Christians everywhere.

Words like *always* and *grace* summon us to complete dependence on the Holy Spirit and draw us to the heart of Jesus. Paul understood that communicating at this depth can only be accomplished successfully as we become intoxicated by God's divine influence.

Can you imagine what our lives and workplaces would be like if our conversations were always full of grace? Our conversations could be used by God to encourage the coworker who feels hopeless and stuck in a deep dark pit. Our words can bring life to others—but if we do not pray, use wisdom, and season our words with grace, they can also bring pain to others by demeaning their values, dreams, or hopes. I know firsthand the power of our words, for I've not always used my words to encourage, uplift, or show God's love as Paul exhorts. Since I can't undo what's already been done, I am now committed to a number of communication essentials.

First, I give God complete control and authority over my tongue, words, and heart. When I'm not obedient in this area, I quickly seek forgiveness and start over again. Then I pray that God would season my words with salt so they are pleasing to his ears. If you cook, you can appreciate the importance of how salt enhances the flavor of most foods. Salt can not only transform food and make it more palatable but also help preserve it. Just as it is rare for a restaurant table not to have salt, Christians should never be without our "salt."

I also continually commit to being in God's Word, knowing that only by his Word can I encourage another person. So often we try to come up with the right words and wrack our brains for that encouraging thing to say when the answer is already laid out in Scripture. Becoming effective and relevant communicators is not about our fancy vocabulary but about relying on what our "communication manual" says. People should say of us what my friend Lisa says: "She's the biggest plagiarizer there is, because she's always using God's words!"

Proverbs 25:11 says, "A word aptly spoken is like apples of gold in settings of silver." As we seek to become messengers of the gospel in the workplace, let's lavishly communicate grace through our words. As Trent Butler wrote, "Grace is the hallmark of the Christian experience. To share in the gospel is to be a partaker of grace."[5] Christians should be looking for opportunities to partake in grace, always seeking to encourage others in the workplace through the spoken word.

The Great Communicator:
The Principle of Love

Paul concludes his passage of instruction with "so that you may know how to answer everyone" (Col. 4:6). I don't know about you, but the only way I will ever be able to accomplish this is with *Christ's love,* our fifth and final communication principle.

Jesus demonstrated love through every word he spoke and every conversation he had. His words ministered healing to hurting people like you and me in every imaginable way: physically, emotionally, and spiritually. He knew how to "answer" everyone—with love. So when Paul concludes this passage with, "so that we may know how to answer everyone," he once again draws us to the heart of Jesus, the Great Communicator.

The Great Communicator always communicated heart to heart, changing lives for eternity. Without Christ's personal demonstration of love, we would be speechless. Despite being women of prayer, truth, wisdom, and grace, if we do not have Christ's love, our communication principles become meaningless rules, powerless and ineffective. These principles only become effective and relevant when they are built upon the chief cornerstone, Jesus Christ himself. When we look at the life of Jesus in the four Gospels, we see before us a fully human man communicating heart to heart with everyone as only a loving Savior is capable of doing.

In the Book of Luke we see Jesus' love for God the Father as he communes with him through prayer. One example of this took place when Jesus was being baptized by John the Baptist: "As [Jesus] was praying, heaven was opened and the Holy Spirit descended on him. . . . And a voice came from heaven: 'You are my Son, whom I love; with you I am well pleased'" (3:21–22). Jesus communed with the Father through prayer, and this intimate exchange of words further demonstrates the power of prayer.

In the Book of Mark we read the account of Jesus before the Sanhedrin, where words are used to hurl false accusations, insults, and a death sentence (Mark 14:53–65). Even when face-to-face with his persecutors, Jesus stands for truth. As the high priest gives Jesus an opportunity to denounce his teachings by asking, "Are you the Christ, the Son of the Blessed One?" Jesus unswervingly speaks the truth, saying, "I am" (Mark 14:61–62), fully aware that his words would seal his death sentence.

Earlier in the story of the life of Jesus, we read about the death of Lazarus (John 11:1–44). In this story Jesus demonstrates heavenly wisdom as he wastes no words when raising Lazarus with the command, "Lazarus, come out!" (John 11:43). I have heard ministers using this passage say that had Jesus not specifically called Lazarus by name, everyone would have been raised from the dead. We will never know, but we do know that by his words he brought forth life.

As we continue reading the Gospels, we come to the chilling account of Jesus on the cross offering that indescribable gift of grace to the criminal hanging beside him (Luke 23:33, 39–43). In the midst of unimaginable suffering, Jesus pours out his love as he says, "I tell you the truth, today you will be with me in paradise" (Luke 23:43). By his mere words a lost soul enters eternal paradise—what amazing grace!

In every conversation, Jesus used each word to show his indisputable love for each person, as we see with his conversation with the woman at the well (John 4:1–26). At the sixth hour—or in modern day language, lunch break—Jesus is sitting down, weary from walking, when a Samaritan woman comes to the well to draw water. As the story unfolds we see Jesus, the Great Communicator, fulfill the law of love by putting aside cultural taboos, predispositions, and religious boundaries to minister truth to a hurting, desperate woman. In many ways she is a reflection of every woman living in emotional and spiritual bondage, because she has not drunk from the "spring of water welling up to eternal life" (v. 14).

Words have eternal power and can alter a life forever, as they did for this woman at the well. From one conversation during lunch break, many lives were changed. As Christians it's only through the holy Word of God that we become effective and relevant communicators of the gospel, transforming our workplaces for Christ. When this happens we give honor and glory to the Father, just as the Son did.

"In the beginning was the Word and the Word was with God and the Word was God" (John 1:1). God sent his Word to us to bring forth life, and we must communicate his words to bring forth light in the workplace.

• • •

Personal Insight

What new truths has God revealed to you? What is God revealing to you about your heart and what two key principles you can apply in order to better communicate with others?

_____

_____

_____

_____

_____

• • •

Spiritual Application

Write out the Scripture verse(s) in this chapter that gave you encouragement for your current work situation. _____

_____

_____

_____

How is God speaking to you through this verse? _____

_____

_____

_____

What workplace actions will you commit to following through on to become an effective and relevant communicator in the workplace? _____

_____

_____

_____

5

Take Heart!

Overcoming Conflict
in the Workplace

I have told you these things, so that in me you may have peace.
In this world you will have trouble. But take heart! I have overcome the world.

John 16:33

Like communication, conflict can be constructive or
destructive. Constructive conflict centers on corporate
issues and resolutions; it is often the catalyst for notable
changes within an organization and in a person. Conversely,
destructive conflict germinates from self-seeking concerns that
are contrary to corporate missions and philosophies; it is the
impetus for dysfunction within a department, low employee
morale, and hostile working environments. It feeds on the life-
line of office politics, gossip, and the grapevine.

We will eventually experience conflict with anyone we interact with on a regular basis. But we have the ability to triumph over conflict because, as 1 John 4:4 tells us, "the one who is in you is greater than the one who is in the world."

However, when we fail to personalize this and other scriptural truths, we quickly get bogged down with despair, distress, and discouragement. Sooner or later, conflict (whether good or bad) adversely affects us emotionally, physically, professionally, and spiritually. Instead of starting our workday with fresh insight and ending it with a sense of accomplishment, we begin it with the chain of dread around our neck and end it with a cloud of defeat looming over us. Let me give you four different examples of how conflict eats away at our being like an infectious disease. See if you recognize any of these characteristics and side effects.

Emotionally Infected by Conflict

The once chatty and friendly coworker no longer talks about personal issues during breaks. She prefers to stick to work-related issues and tasks at hand—only! Conflict has infected her, leaving her emotionally expended. She believes the only way she can survive her hostile work environment is to be guarded, so that's exactly what she does. In an attempt to protect herself from the emotional pain and hurt stemming from conflict, she guards her heart from the source of conflict and hides her once vulnerable, friendly self. All anyone can say is, "She's just not herself."

Physically Infected by Conflict

A reliable employee suddenly begins calling in sick, showing up to work late, and leaving early. Unlike other employees who abuse their sick leave by calling in sick every Friday or Monday, this employee has an excellent reputation and is known for exhibiting a strong work ethic.

Most likely she's coping with ongoing, stressful issues within the workplace and feels that her only recourse is to withdraw physically from the source of conflict—in this case, it's work. She refuses to be controlled by her work environment and therefore maintains "control" with her absence. All anyone can say is, "We just don't understand her."

Professionally Infected by Conflict

This employee is constantly hunting for a new job but never finds one. Whenever a dispute erupts, she searches all the more. Once the conflict subsides, so does her desire to leave.

This employee bases her professional decisions on what's going on in her work environment. The conflict in her work environment has become a measuring stick for her happiness, replacing her sense of professional well-being. All anyone can say is, "I don't know why she can't find a job."

Spiritually Infected by Conflict

This is the most devastating result of conflict because it causes the employee to lose hope and become stagnant in life and on the job. This employee isn't able to move beyond the "Why me, Lord?" feelings, so she resentfully but respectfully shows up to work, does what's expected, and then clocks out not a minute later than quitting time. All the while she harbors bitterness in her heart against the company, her boss, her coworkers, and God.

Work conflict has infected her sense of spiritual well-being because she's lost her inner joy and has quietly given up her hope for living victoriously in the workplace. Now she's resigned herself to just making the best of her workweek until Friday rolls around. All anyone can say is, "I don't think she likes her job, but she's nice."

Infected or Affecting

Have you been infected in any of these areas? Like you, I've sometimes allowed my workplace wounds to become infected. I've popped my pills (Tums, that is), pulled my hair out (figuratively), and prayed my prayers ("Please send a snow day!").

Having spent over a decade in human resources, I've seen conflict erupt at all levels within a company: between employee and employee, between employer and employee, between management and staff, and between management and management. You name it, and most likely I've seen it, heard it, or prayed about it. Yet I'm still grappling to be victorious in my own life over this thing called conflict or trouble. Living according to our faith and victoriously overcoming conflict in the workplace is complex! Any Christian who gives a quick fix or "church" answer for dealing with these complex issues in today's workplace only minimizes the struggle.

The truth of the matter is, the Christian life is *hard*. Yes, hard! I didn't say it first—Scripture does. Take a look at just three passages written to believers and see for yourself:

> Consider it pure joy, my brothers, whenever you face trials of many kinds, because you know that the testing of your faith develops perseverance.
>
> James 1:2–3

> I consider that our present sufferings are not worth comparing with the glory that will be revealed in us.
>
> Romans 8:18

But if you suffer for doing good and you endure it, this is commendable before God. To this you were called, because Christ suffered for you, leaving you an example, that you should follow in his steps.

1 Peter 2:20–21

Since Christ, the Son of God, endured trials, conflicts, and hardships of all kinds, I have no doubt that we will suffer on two accounts: First, by the mere fact that we live in a sinful, fallen world, everyone is subjected to pain and suffering. Second, we will suffer for the sake of Christ's name. Trials and Christianity go hand in hand, but if we give our trials to God, they can be a good thing—as James shows us, trials develop perseverance, and perseverance makes us mature and complete (James 1:2–4).

I recently heard a believer who is suffering from cancer say, "We only experience the true essence of God's abundance when everything—and I mean everything!—seems hopelessly impossible, yet inwardly we feel his love, peace, and joy. This is the abundant life! God's abundance comes at a cost." I believe the abundance she was referring to was spiritual maturity and completeness such as she came to experience through trusting God in an impossible situation.

Christ suffered through many hardships and affected countless lives for the kingdom of God. With him by our sides, we too can affect others instead of being infected.

The Roots of Conflict

The best way to avoid being infected by conflict is to be aware of how conflict often begins. Let's look at three common sources of workplace conflict: politics, the office grapevine, and office slander, all of which can be part of everyday work life—if you let them.

Conflict Based on Politics

Everyone has a story about injustices that stem from "politics," be it office, family, or some other kind of politics. Most decisions based on politics lead to injustices of all kinds, as we see in the story of Joseph, the son of Jacob and Rachel, told in Genesis 37–41.

From the beginning Joseph gets preferential treatment from his parents, including the richly ornamented robe his father gave him. Because of this his brothers hated him, and in an attempt to kill him they throw Joseph in a pit, then sell him into slavery.

Eventually Joseph ends up working for one of Pharaoh's officials, Potiphar. While working in Potiphar's home, he is falsely accused of rape (sexual harassment on the job) and thrown into jail. Rotting away in jail for "just doing his job" and upholding a standard of integrity, he interprets a dream for a chief cupbearer.

The interpretation is both favorable and accurate. Joseph also tells the chief cupbearer, "But when all goes well with you, remember me and show me kindness; mention me to Pharaoh and get me out of this prison" (Gen. 40:14). But the chief cupbearer forgets Joseph, and two years slowly pass.

Have you ever helped another employee, possibly your boss, out of an impossible situation, yet when promotion or salary increase time rolls around, he or she completely forgets your efforts? Your hard work is forgotten, possibly year after year, like Joseph. Time slowly ticks by for you. You pray for justice to prevail, but it appears God has forgotten you. It's hard not to think of yourself rotting away at your cubicle or in your office imagining what your career would be like had this or that not happened.

Conflict Based on the Office Grapevine

Unfortunately the company grapevine keeps most of us entangled in the ongoing conflict within the workplace. If we do not guard our mouths, ears, and hearts, we too can be easily pulled into its web, adding to the confusion, commotion, and conflict that feeds off this vine.

Drug testing has become a common workplace practice in today's corporate climate. As such, the company I worked for made it mandatory that all potential employees receive a drug screening test prior to their first day of work. Needless to say, we had lots of paperwork to process. So I assigned an employee from my department the responsibility of handling the process and then forwarding the confidential results to me.

Anytime you have information this juicy, it's bound to come out in the office grapevine, even though you set up barriers to fight against it. Wouldn't you know it? The confidential information was mysteriously being rerouted to another department, and within weeks it became painstakingly clear that this sensitive and confidential information had been discussed with others at great length. The grapevine had reared its ugly head and the test results of an employee had been compromised. My heart ached because this employee hadn't even started her first day, yet her privacy was violated.

Have you ever betrayed another coworker by passing along their secret? Or have you confided in someone, shared your heart with someone, or discussed a sensitive work issue, only to hear whispers later on?

Conflict Based on Office Slander

Have you ever had a lunch appointment that turned out to be the worst hour of your career? You guessed it, I have! I once had the assignment of revamping a company-wide benefit program. The current program was with a vendor the company had used for years. However, after much research, we chose to go with another company to handle those services. After this decision was made, I contacted the current vendor and discussed the change. At the vendor's suggestion I agreed to meet with his assistant for lunch to follow up on the administrative details of changing from his company to another. Lunch went well, or so I thought until my boss came to my office and questioned the conversation, my character, and my overall commitment to the company based on what he had heard happened at lunch.

Has someone ever told a blatant lie about you, yet no matter how much you protest, your defense falls on deaf ears? Or have you ever felt the pain of someone questioning your work ethics and character? Imagine how I felt when untrue things were said about me by a person attempting to slander my character.

Victory Triumphs over Conflict

I purposely omitted the ending of each story to illustrate the harsh realities of conflict in the workplace and to demonstrate the angst that conflict can bring to our everyday lives. Too often as Christians we wrap life's struggles in neat little packages, unfolding the problem and solution in poignant paragraphs as though this is life itself.

In reality, life is not so predictable as a paragraph may suggest. It's quite the contrary, as most of us would agree. We know the anguish and pain of dealing with conflict. The resolution process is sometimes longer than we believe we can endure. We may suffer for a period of months and even years before we experience our breakthrough.

Conflict is taxing, requiring perseverance. Paul says this about suffering in Romans 5:3–4: "We also rejoice in our sufferings, because we know that suffering produces perseverance; perseverance, character; and character, hope." There is no quick and easy solution to overcoming workplace conflict. But as believers we have hope!

Victory over Politics

Joseph did indeed endure imprisonment for a long period of time. But as his story unfolds in Genesis 41, we see hope! No one, not even Joseph, could have imagined what was about to take place as Pharaoh summoned him from jail to interpret his dream.

Remember, two years had passed from the time the chief cupbearer was released until now, when Joseph meets with Pharaoh to interpret his dream. Pharaoh provides Joseph with the details of his dream, and Joseph replies, "I cannot do it . . . but God will give Pharaoh the answers he desires" (Gen. 41:16).

I love the fact that Joseph doesn't lament about the injustices of his life, as I would have, but rather displays humility, exalts God, and then gives Pharaoh strategic plans for leading his nation through the seven years of abundance and then of famine in the land.

Pharaoh is taken with Joseph's discernment and wisdom and asks, "Can we find anyone like this man, one in whom is the spirit of God?" (Gen. 41:38). Pharaoh then places Joseph in charge of all Egypt, dresses him in fine linens, and even gives him his signet ring.

God brings victory to Joseph and blesses him well beyond his expectation by elevating him from being a prisoner of circumstances to a man of power, authority, and generational influence. Joseph's dream as a young boy is being fulfilled now that he is a man because he knows and works for the Great Politician who rules the universe.

Victory over the Grapevine

I struggled with how to approach the department manager about the clear violations of drug testing confidentiality and employee privacy. But I laid my fears aside and brought it up, emphasizing the importance of employee confidentiality and making it clear that all results were to come straight to my office—no exceptions!

After our conversation I felt a burden lifted, even though I knew my reputation for not being a "team player" would be the next hot topic of discussion.

I received a lot of grief about isolating myself from the "in" crowd and taking work too seriously. Yet I determined not to buckle under the peer pressure of the "in" crowd and distanced myself from the office grapevine.

My prayer was that God would watch over me in the midst of uncertainty and great pressure to conform. And he did! Not only did he sustain me during many stressful encounters, but I believe I influenced my workplace by standing on the principles of truth.

Victory over Slander

"Dinner?" I asked in a surprised voice, "I'll have to get back with you." How could this person who had said so many negative things about me want to join me for dinner? His assistant had slandered my good name! As soon as I could catch my breath, I sat down and called my husband, Kevin. "You are not going to believe who just called us for dinner! Yes, you heard correctly! He wants you and me to join him and his wife for dinner."

Needless to say I was not jumping at the thought. The previous week's lunch engagement had cured me for life. But after consulting with Kevin and doing lots of praying, we accepted the invitation and joined them at an exclusive country club in town (his treat!).

I never received a formal apology, but I know beyond a shadow of a doubt that God restored my reputation and proved the truth about what had happened. My hope was in what God had accomplished, and that was good enough for me.

Spiritual Armor for the Workplace

Most of us have similar or worse stories to tell about struggling to overcome conflict in the workplace. Yet with every story, God has a unique plan in place so we can experience victory for ourselves and see his faithfulness in our lives.

No matter how our various workplace conflicts are resolved, in order for us to triumph over them, we all have to do one thing: put on the armor of God's truth. Suiting up for battle isn't easy, but it is necessary.

Unlike other soldiers preparing for war, we know who's won our battle. There's no second-guessing. Even when the enemy takes us by surprise with office politics, the grapevine, slander, or interpersonal conflict, we can rest assured that he will never take God by surprise. No one can launch a surprise attack on our Commander in Chief.

In John 16:33 Jesus exhorts believers with the promise of *peace, encouragement,* and *victory* to overcome the world's troubles. Resting in these promises is a by-product of knowing Christ as Lord and Savior. Apart from knowing him, we are unable to acquire these promises, but as we abide in him, we receive and experience his peace, encouragement, and victory as his gift to us. These promises act as armor to shield us from the wounds conflict can inflict on us.

The Armor of Peace

The word *peace* used in this passage comes from the Greek word *eirēnē*, which means "quietness and rest."[1] It corresponds with the Hebrew word *shalom* (a word familiar to most of us), which expresses "the idea of peace, well-being, restoration, reconciliation with God and salvation in the fullest sense; freedom from distress and fear."[2]

The very idea of being "reconciled with God" blows my mind, yet this is what Jesus promises the believer. Understanding peace in this light should free us from the agitation and unrest we experience in conflict.

Peace is the first piece of armor we must put on as we step into our respective offices and work environments. Only with the armor of peace can we find shelter from the conflict that wages war against us. What an awesome privilege and gift to be reconciled with God the Father and be free from worry, fear, and the sin that chokes the life out of us.

As we put on the armor of Christ's peace, my prayer is this: "May the God of hope fill you with all joy and peace as you trust in him, so that you may overflow with hope by the power of the Holy Spirit" (Rom. 15:13) in the midst of conflict.

The Armor of Encouragement

Encouragement, or in this passage to "take heart," comes from the Greek word for cheer, *tharseō*, which means, "to have courage: be of good cheer (comfort); to have boldness."[3]

This boldness from God enables us to stare conflict in the eye and declare, "We are hard pressed on every side, but not crushed; perplexed, but not in despair; persecuted, but not abandoned; struck down, but not destroyed" (2 Cor. 4:8–9). We can do this with confidence because we know that God's will transcends our own abilities and tramples the devil and his tactics under Christ's feet.

Think for a moment about someone you esteem highly as an encourager. No matter what's going on in her life, she has an encouraging word to impart for your life. She says just the right thing at the right time. No wonder you love being around her! Now take this person's ability to encourage you and magnify it one zillion times. This becomes the beginning of what Christ does when he encourages us to take heart!

As we armor ourselves with Christ's encouragement, my prayer is that you would not be discouraged by your trials, but rather strengthened and encouraged in your faith (1 Thess. 3:2–3) in the midst of conflict.

The Armor of Victory

The word *victory* or *overcome* comes from the Greek word *nikaō*, meaning "to subdue, conquer, overcome, prevail, get the victory."[4] This is great news: Jesus overcame the world; he prevailed; he got the victory! We need to start reveling in this awesome, powerful truth ourselves.

Our triumph is in Christ's victory over sin, the world, and death. The war is already fought *and* won; we simply need to march onto the battlefield next to the one who's overcome and do our victory dance—kind of like the football player who scores a touchdown! Christ's victory on the cross and triumph over the world should incite us to dance, shout, and scream "Hallelujah!" in the first, second, third, and fourth quarters of the devil's game.

As we put on the armor of Christ's victory, my prayer is that we would know that "we are more than conquerors through him who loved us" (Rom. 8:37) and we are on the winner's side.

Standing on God's Truth

Many of us are wearing the armor and ready to declare our alliance with God, but when push comes to shove, we run for cover. Why is that? I think it is because we don't really trust our Commander in Chief, and as much as we want to, trust seems impossible—especially when the enemy is staring us down.

Standing on God's truth as the enemy attempts to devour us is a daunting challenge for most of us. We desire to move beyond doubt and stand unwavering on God's Word. We see others doing it and wonder in amazement. But how do we move into the realm of confidence in this truth for ourselves?

My personal journey to victory started with an in-depth study of God's Word, expanding on what I explained in chapter 2. Only after I starting studying God's Word for myself, digging into commentaries and Bible dictionaries and praying for God to reveal his truth, did I begin to experience personal victory even in the midst of conflict.

Once you begin digging into the Word and praying, you'll discover truth for yourself. You'll discover the truth that "All Scripture is God-breathed and is useful for teaching, rebuking, correcting and training in righteousness, so that the man of God may be thoroughly equipped for every good work" (2 Tim. 3:16–17). You'll understand the power of God's "divinely breathed" words. Fully understanding this verse will transform your life. The evidence will be seen in your:

- attitude about Scripture (it is the inspiration of God)
- approach to life (everything God requires of us, he equips us for)
- actions as a Christian (Scripture teaches, corrects, and trains us for the journey)

As we study God's Word, our feelings and our faith will come into line. Truth from his Word transforms our feelings of uncertainty to living in faith with certainty. Standing on God's Word is best. His truth is what will allow you to stand on the battlefield in the midst of slinging mud and poisonous darts and still walk away in victory.

Walking with the Holy Spirit

When a manager greets you at 7:30 in the morning with, "Do you have a minute?" you know it's not going to be just a minute, and most likely the problem will take the remaining day to digest, let alone solve. When this happened to me, I was right!

One of the manager's employees had been thrown into jail and had telephoned in a "sick" day. No one knew how to handle the situation. What was I to do? Like any sane person, I cried out, "Lord ... *please!*" Those of you who have been there know that "please" is the condensed version of "Lord, I absolutely, positively, without a doubt cannot do this! You are going to have to get me through this . . . please, Lord . . . please!"

To handle uncharted problems like this, we must draw our strength from the Holy Spirit. In John 14:26 Jesus says, "The Counselor, the Holy Spirit, whom the Father will send in my name, will teach you all things and will remind you of everything"—and I needed reminding again of why I was working there.

As we anchor ourselves to the Holy Spirit, we become enabled to handle the day-to-day challenges that await each of us. *He* is our strength. That's why all of this New Age talk about "finding your inner self" and "being esteemed in yourself" makes little sense to me. Personally, I don't want *my* finite strength to be the whole source of strength for anything I'm facing, let alone for overcoming personal conflict and spiritual warfare. As we relinquish our independence for dependence on the Holy Spirit, we can walk through the "fire" and not be burned (Isa. 43:2) because he is with us. Walking like a victor in the midst of the battle will require unwavering dependence on the Holy Spirit for our strength, insight, and wisdom.

Running with Jesus Christ

Lastly, when we go onto the battlefield we need to be prepared to go the distance. As Hebrews 12:1–2 says, "let us run with perseverance the race marked out for us. Let us fix our eyes on Jesus, the author and perfecter of our faith."

My family went to the 1996 summer Olympic Games in Atlanta. It was an awesome experience to sit only rows from the greatest athletes in the world. And despite the talents of the gold medal winners, the most remarkable person to me was a female distance runner from Africa. I'll always remember her personal triumph in the face of overwhelming obstacles. Despite being at least two laps behind all the other athletes and the last one left on the track, she persevered.

Initially the crowd felt sorry for her, but after seeing her resolve, people from all countries began applauding her. As she finished the race, the crowd gave her a standing ovation. She didn't take home the gold, silver, or bronze medal, but she tasted personal victory as she crossed the finish line. Just as she ran the race set out before her, we too need to run the race set out before us.

The Message translates Hebrews 12:1–2 as, "Keep your eyes on Jesus, who both began and finished this race we're in. Study how he did it. Because he never lost sight of where he was headed—that exhilarating finish in and with God— he could put up with anything along the way: cross, shame, whatever. And now he's *there,* in the place of honor, right alongside God. When you find yourselves flagging in your faith, go over that story again, item by item, that long litany of hostility he plowed through. *That* will shoot adrenaline into your souls!"

Running the victory lap in the midst of a battle that appears to be lost will require fixing our eyes on Jesus and not our circumstances. And the truth is, he'll carry us if we ask him.

Kneeling as a Peacemaker

There are only three ingredients to being a peacemaker in the workplace: prayer, prayer, and prayer! Unlike other recipes, the first ingredient is just as important as the second and the third. We need all parts; none can be omitted.

Apart from prayer, we will not succeed at overcoming conflict. In every situation mentioned throughout this chapter, prayer was the common denominator: I prayed, someone prayed, or we prayed. As E. M. Bounds wrote, "The Word of God is made effectual and operative by the process and practice of prayer."[5] We all need to practice prayer in and out of the workplace.

This was never truer than when my husband, Kevin, was in the army and worked for a senior officer. It was clear from the first time Kevin overheard his boss's conversation with another senior officer that his boss was making him the "fall guy." In light of the ensuing problems, we began to do something radical—we started praying for Kevin's boss. Every Wednesday we would seek God's favor and blessings for him and his family. We were desperate, and Scripture says, "Love your enemies and pray for those who persecute you" (Matt. 5:44). So that's exactly what we did for over six months.

And wouldn't you know it, it worked! Although Kevin's work environment remained hostile, we personally witnessed a radical change in his boss's heart, demonstrated through words of reconciliation prior to his boss's retirement. As Christians we need to be peacemakers at all times but especially when others are undermining us emotionally, professionally, physically, and spiritually. Peacemakers are needed during wartime and we are at war!

I leave you with two verses concerning conflict in the office: "In fact, everyone who wants to live a godly life in Christ Jesus will be persecuted" (2 Tim. 3:12), and "But the Lord is faithful, and he will strengthen and protect you from the evil one" (2 Thess. 3:3). Remember these words when you need encouragement to overcome conflict in the workplace in a godly way.

• • •

Personal Insight

What new truths has God revealed to you in the midst of your current situation? What steps will you take to walk victoriously through your workplace conflict? _____

_____

_____

_____

• • •

Spiritual Application

Write out the Scripture verse(s) in this chapter that gave you encouragement for your current work situation. _____

_____

_____

_____

How is God speaking to you through this verse? _____

_____

_____

_____

What workplace actions will you commit to following through on as you strive to overcome conflict in the workplace so God is glorified? _____

_____

_____

_____

6

Encouraged
in Heart, United
in Love

God's Purpose for Work

My purpose is that they may be encouraged in heart and united in love, so that they may have the full riches of complete understanding, in order that they may know the mystery of God, namely, Christ.

Colossians 2:2

I was especially excited to write this chapter for two reasons: it was the genesis of my journey to experiencing victory in the workplace, and it was the catalyst for writing this book. Understanding God's purpose in the workplace was my saving grace, embracing his purpose was my shelter from the world's trappings of "success," and committing to his purpose was my armor from the enemy's destructive schemes.

This chapter is my heart's passion unfolding word by word and the most important message of this book. As you continue on this journey, please don't skip over or leaf through these pages. The Chief Executive Officer of the universe has a great purpose for your career that includes:

- understanding his divine purpose for your workweek
- working in harmony with him as an employee of the gospel
- experiencing lasting victory in your workplace
- rejoicing over the new life of a coworker

Enough said—let's dig in! The apostle Paul says, "Whatever you do, work at it with all your heart, as working for the Lord, not for men. . . . It is the Lord Christ you are serving" (Col. 3:23–24). The dictionary defines work as "physical or mental activity undertaken to achieve a purpose."[1] That's no doubt a good description, especially as we consider the word *purpose*, yet compared to the original Greek meaning, it's incomplete. The word *work* in this passage comes from the Greek word *ergazomai*, which means "to toil, be *engaged in* or with, to commit, do, labor for, *minister about*, work" (italics mine).[2]

Does this remind you of anything? When I first read this definition, I immediately thought of marriage. Could working for the Lord possibly be comparable to a marriage partnership? After all, marriage requires many, if not all, of the same activities. Considering this, I began to reflect on my work partnership with the Lord. For instance, would the Lord say I am engaged with him, committed to him, laboring for him, ministering about him, and ultimately married to working for him?

If working with the Lord is likened to a marriage partnership—with him being the head—could I declare myself faithful, or was I adulterous? All I could think of was the many times I did not love, honor, and obey the very one who chose me to partner with him, serve him, and do his work. Indeed, I had committed adultery every time I reached beyond his will in an attempt to gain personal recognition, status, and ambition.

Truth came to light and I cried, "Forgive me, Lord!" God's primary purpose for giving us our careers is not about any of those *things*—although it may include them—but about his love, his power, his glory, and ultimately about his Son. Somewhere along the way I had forsaken the responsibilities as spelled out in my "Employment Letter of Agreement."

Such a letter is simply a written agreement from the company to the new employee outlining starting date, salary, title, benefits, and usually a brief description of job responsibilities. For all intents and purposes, it's proof of the mutual obligations joining employer and employee together.

Similarly, God has written an "Employment Letter of Agreement" for believers in the workplace. It reads differently, but it's our "proof" that we are working for him and reads something like this:

Beloved Daughter,

Welcome to My Kingdom Come, Inc. I'm rejoicing over your decision to accept a position as Employee of the Gospel. I have great plans for your life, plans to prosper you and give you a hope and a future (Jeremiah 29:11). I just ask that you place your hopes and dreams in my hands.

You will learn much in this position, but most important is my mission, that all people would be saved and come to a knowledge of the truth (1 Tim. 2:4). Always keep this truth tucked in the depths of your heart, and you will remain on course with my will and purpose: for you to represent my Son to all I place in your path.

I have blessed you with great knowledge, skills, and abilities to enable you to succeed at all you do. However, more necessary than succeeding is demonstrating my love to others in the workplace. Love lavishly as I have loved you (John 13:34). Show kindness, be gentle, extend patience, and provide comfort to all I place in your workday—no one is exempt! Your colleagues need to experience my love and accept the indescribable gift of my only Son so they can have everlasting life (John 3:16).

In your own strength this seems impossible, and indeed it is. But do not fret; I've given you the Holy Spirit. He will help you in all your weakness (Rom. 8:26), making my mission possible! Whenever you feel weary, timid, or unable to carry on, just come directly to the Executive Office. No need to make an appointment or see if I'm available, for I am always here and my door is always open to you. As you approach my throne you will find grace to help you in your time of need (Heb. 4:16). Here you will be refreshed.

Love,
Sufficient Grace

Unlike other Employment Letters of Agreement, God signed his name in blood. The question to you remains: "Will you sign on the dotted line and make this a binding partnership?"

Ministry in the Workplace

Have you ever thought, "I'm just not bold enough to talk about Christ with my coworkers"? What about, "I'm here to work, get paid, and go home—and to be honest, I'm struggling just to do that"? Or finally, *"That's* not my calling." I'm just going to assume you are nodding or at least smiling.

Most of us have thought or spoken similar words despite Jesus' Great Commission, "Go into all the world and preach the good news to all creation" (Mark 16:15). At first glance it's easy to dismiss the literal command to preach because we often place this responsibility on our pastor, an evangelist, or a person called to missions work.

Surprisingly, the word *preach* means to proclaim divine truth (the gospel), and in turn *proclaim* means to publicly or officially announce. This is ministry at its core: a public and official announcement of our love for the gospel of Jesus Christ. Surely we can all do this. Nothing to it! But then again, if it's so easy, why aren't we doing it?

I believe the problem stems in part from our unwillingness, fear, lack of spiritual knowledge, and disobedience—just to name a few. Regardless of the excuse or reason we give, Jesus summed up our problem in a nutshell: "The harvest is plentiful but the workers are few" (Matt. 9:37).

As I considered my own situation, I had to face some hard truths about myself. I was a complacent Christian. The sacrifice seemed too great. I was self-centered. I did a lot of the "right" things in the workplace but rarely Christ-honoring things.

After years of working ten-plus hours a day and giving my all, gaping holes began to appear in my life. I felt unappreciated, used up, and trapped in my so-called "good" career. There had to be more to working—I hoped, I prayed, I begged!

The thought of "just making it through the week" weighed me down like a cast iron chain around my neck. Only after seeking the counsel of my pastor and making some radical decisions about my life did I begin to emerge from the darkness that overshadowed my workplace. Change was slow but lasting, especially as I allowed God's truth to transform my life. I gradually saw the benefits of resigning my will and ways for his purpose and plans for my career and ministry in the workplace. Taking hold of God's ordained purpose for me brought new hope, faith, and endurance to withstand the ongoing stress, office politics, work overload . . . everything! Talk about a life-changing epiphany—this was mine.

My already-spent paycheck, so-called impressive title, and fleeting status took its proper place behind God's beautifully designed plan. I still had ambitions for career opportunities, financial compensation, and advancement in my field; however, my perspective and allegiance shifted. In light of God's purpose for me, these were no longer of chief importance.

When given the opportunity to share God's truth, I did. When work situations seemed to spin out of control, I sought God through prayer, usually in the quietness of my office. I began praying for coworkers faithfully and specifically. I took time to slow down. The biggest difference was becoming conscientious about making my life Christlike: smiling and saying hello, showing genuine concern, completely depending on the Holy Spirit to enable me throughout the day, and representing Christ in my workplace through my attitude, actions, and approach. My time in the workplace became a precious commodity.

To put into perspective how many opportunities God provided me to share the gospel I might have missed if my perspective had not changed, consider this: I spent 17 years as a part- or full-time employee. Multiply 17 years by 240 days, which is the number of days worked in a year excluding vacation, holiday, and sick time, and you get 4,080 days. I interacted with at least 5 people each day, so 5 people multiplied by 4,080 days equals 20,400 opportunities to share the gospel.

Even if we cut that figure in half—let's call it God's grace—I had possibly overlooked 10,200 opportunities to share the gospel!

I'm amazed that God has graciously allowed me so many opportunities to share the gift of his Son on my little mission field called the workplace. Hypothetically speaking, if this was a test for workplace ministry, I would have flunked—even on the curve!

Just as the hopeless crowds followed Christ around during his time of ministry on earth, many more are following us around in the workplace searching for truth. Our responsibility is to point them to Jesus Christ. This is our commission from him and our commitment to him. Anything less sabotages his will for our work life.

Ministry in the workplace is a step of faith, an act of obedience, and a walk of love we must all make if we want to work for the CEO of the universe. As we start each new day, let's commit to making it a day of ministry for the Lord.

Where Ministry Begins

Don't be deceived by thoughts like "It's too late to start now," "People will think I'm a hypocrite," or "I'll just wait until my next job." I remember thinking just those thoughts and for a period of time being immobilized by them. But these are all lies from the devil, the father of lies (John 8:44), who would like nothing better than for you to come under his condemnation. The truth is, God is not limited by time, so it's never too late.

Ministry in the workplace is about trusting him with all the nuances of the workplace. Our responsibility is to *reach up* and *reach out!* First and most importantly, we must reach up to the Lord for his strength, power, assurance, and grace. If we fail to do this, we will be burdened down with worry and feel like we have to muster up the confidence, fake the know-how, or pass the test. Soon we will be drained like an overcooked spaghetti noodle—limp and tasteless.

Second Corinthians 3:5 says, "Not that we are competent in ourselves to claim anything for ourselves, but our competence comes from God." It's only through him that we are able to do what he has prepared for us to do in the workplace. And it's only through his Spirit that others will be affected and we will experience life on the job. Our competence to minister God's truth in the workplace must come from him. The word *competent* in this verse comes from the Greek word *hikanos* and means "as if coming in season . . . ample (in amount) or fit (in character): able, content, enough, good, great . . . security, sufficient, worthy."[3] How liberating to know that God has made us fit, sufficient, able, *and* worthy to do all he's calling us to do.

Apart from depending on his Spirit working in us, we will never be competent to accomplish his purpose in our own effort (Gal. 3:3), no matter how self-motivated we think we are. All attempts to be self-sufficient are futile. Only after God's truth is embedded in our own life do we experience truth for ourselves and become effective employees of the gospel. Compare this to me telling you about my friend Noni, a fabulous portrait artist. I've seen her work and know her ability to make canvas come alive with color. Yet until you marvel at her work personally, you are unlikely to value her abilities. No matter how much I write or what others say about God's purpose, until you experience it personally, my words are useless.

As Henry Blackaby says, "There's nothing more appealing or convincing to a watching world than to hear the testimony of someone who has just been with Jesus."[4] This leads us to reaching out to others.

A gift that remains unopened benefits no one—even the recipient—regardless of how priceless it is. We must unwrap the precious and rare gift of Jesus Christ for others. Workplace ministry requires that we reach out to others in ways that demonstrate love—not ours but Christ's.

Does this mean you shouldn't reach out until you receive the "Employee of the Month" award? Definitely not, but it does require consistency and commitment. We can't be Sweet Sally one minute and then Sour Suzie the next. James 3:9–10 tells us not to praise God with our mouth in one breath and then curse man in the next.

Behavior that's contrary to representing Christ destroys our testimonies and makes a mockery of the gospel. We are responsible as representatives of Christ in and out of the workplace to live in righteousness and in accordance with God's Word. This is reaching out!

As we pursue righteousness and truth, we will be given endless opportunities to reach out to our coworkers in countless ways. Reaching out is not a method but a ministry of Christlike concern and consideration for the individual so that God is glorified.

My girlfriend's husband, Laurence, has been known to pray with his coworkers and staff. My friend Lina sends encouraging correspondence to a colleague. I believe that in each situation God is glorified because the person reaching out has a genuine love and concern for the other person. Ministry in the workplace begins with God and ends with God. We are just his workers. Scripture says, "The man who plants and the man who waters have one purpose. . . . For we are God's fellow workers" (1 Cor. 3:8–9).

Sharing Your Testimony and the Gospel

You've planted or watered the seed. Now comes the challenging part: sharing your testimony and the gospel of Jesus Christ. What's the difference? Your testimony is your life story, a personal account of Christ living in you. It has a beginning and an end: life before Christ and life after Christ.

The gospel, on the other hand, is the story of Jesus Christ, our Savior, the Son of God. The gospel is about God, the Alpha and the Omega, the beginning and the end. The gospel saves; we need to be saved. The gospel is the living water; we need water. The gospel is about our Creator; we are his creation. The differences between testimony and gospel are stark and indisputable.

Don't get me wrong, our testimonies are powerful, but more powerful is the love of Jesus Christ—and as employees of the gospel we must share both.

I'll be the first to admit that sharing one's testimony is no easy task, especially when many of us are used to hiding behind our "professional" masks. The very thought of sharing what God saved us from and what he's doing in our lives somehow seems too personal to discuss in the workplace.

Just thinking about being this vulnerable with a controlling boss, disrespectful staff member, or competitive colleague is enough to make anyone run for cover. These were my initial battles, but then I asked myself, "If Christians don't share God's truth, who will?" Bosses, coworkers, and colleagues need to know about Christ's love just as much as the person on the streetcorner.

I remember when I first started sharing my testimony as a single woman in the workplace. It was, well, *scary!* And that doesn't even factor in how I felt when faced with the infamous

stare. Was I getting my point across or making a fool of myself?
But sharing my testimony was about my obedience and
acknowledging Christ in my life—everything else was up to
him! After taking myself out of the equation, my anxiety for
saying just the right thing, having all the answers, or won-
dering how compelling my testimony was became his to bear.

To this day I still quake in my boots when it comes to sharing my testimony, especially with people who have sized me
up as being a certain way. The difference is that now I've
learned to depend on the Holy Spirit to enable me to carry
out this awesome and often overwhelming step of faith.

Sharing your personal testimony isn't about achieving per-
fection, putting together a perfect speech, or auditioning for
a part. It's about being led by the Holy Spirit, stepping out in
faith, and honestly and humbly expressing God's goodness,
grace, and gift of new life. There's no formula or best time to
share one's testimony except to follow the leading of the Holy
Spirit.

Recently at a writers' conference a Christian woman shared
with me how another believer prayed in her office. I thought
that was great—until she came to the part about the woman
praying so loudly that it distracted other employees and they
began to make a mockery of her belief. People want to hear a
good story, but more importantly they want to *watch* a good
story. Christ in your life is your testimony, so you don't need
to beat others over the head with loud prayers, words of condemnation, or self-righteousness. Your testimony shouldn't
make a mockery of Christ in your life.

As my friend and Bible study teacher Cynthia says, "Successful witnessing begins with taking the initiative to talk
about the plan of salvation." "He is life" is the best starting
place for sharing the gospel. People will never listen to the
Good News unless we speak. Our coworkers need to hear the

Good News that "God so loved the world that he gave his one and only Son" (John 3:16). This is the gospel! Yet most of us never extend this opportunity of a lifetime, the opportunity for eternal life. Once again, we have to stop and ask ourselves where we would be today if no one had taken the time to share the gospel of Jesus Christ with us.

God has us in our places of work for this very reason. However, we must step out in the faith and boldness that come from the Lord. We can be assured that as we speak the Word of God, we do not need to be afraid because he is with us (Acts 18:9–11). God is able; are you willing?

Share the gift of salvation with someone soon. Don't become intimidated by the "what ifs" or the "how tos." As a young believer I learned the "ABCs of salvation": *admit* you are a sinner (Rom. 3:23), *believe* in your heart that Christ died for your sins (1 Cor. 15:3), and *confess* with your mouth that Christ is Lord, and you will be saved (Rom. 10:9). I continue to use this method of explaining the gospel.

Everyone should be given the same opportunity for eternal life that you and I were given—the opportunity to know Christ as Lord. The gospel is a simple message about the greatest love story ever told. Let's stop muddying it up with all our stuff and start telling it!

Mentoring in the Workplace

Was that section serious or what? Now let's move to something we all need or desire: a mentor. How much sweeter could life be if we all had someone to walk side by side with us in this journey called life? As Christian women we can make a huge impact in the workplace because we can provide both spiritual and professional mentoring to other women, saved and unsaved.

Kathleen Shaw, the first woman to mentor me professionally, will always hold a special place in my life. She extended herself totally, displaying authentic love, concern, and interest in me when my confidence wavered as a new college graduate. She coached me in basic administrative and business etiquette skills, preparing me for future endeavors. Our relationship flourished despite racial, spiritual, and professional differences.

Over the years God has blessed me with other spiritual and professional mentors who have impacted my life enormously. Because of their commitment to nurture, love, and often challenge me, I'm a better wife, mom, professional, and, most importantly, Christian woman today.

Because all women are different, mentoring does not have one set of rules to follow. Nonetheless, I believe these three elements are important in any mentoring relationship: listening, boundaries, and resources.

Listening

As Danny Lehmann wrote, "Sometimes we need to earn the right to speak to a person by giving them a hearing ear."[5] I'll be the first to admit that this is an area God is still refining in my life. Unlike my friend Laryssa, who's gifted at listening *and* phenomenal at recalling, I can hardly remember what my husband and I talked about at breakfast.

One day as we were talking, Laryssa reminded me of a statement I made over a year ago. How did she remember the details of our conversation? After she finished with the "I said, you said," I asked how she could remember so much, and she simply replied, "I just listen."

I had thought of myself as a good listener, but as I considered her words I realized that she listens with her heart, hanging on every word with a desire to understand. I, on the other hand, was hanging on every word just waiting to interject a new thought.

James 1:19 says, *"Take note* of this: Everyone should be quick to listen, slow to speak" (italics mine). When a statement begins like that, we need to stand at attention, ready to take action.

For instance, as I sat on my porch talking with Sue, a wonderful mentor, about being a better Christian, she "stood at attention," listening intently to my heart. Not until I was finished pouring out my heart did she offer me great advice about my many concerns. With great gentleness she said, "Sit still and listen to God. Just spend time with him. Say nothing, just listen!" Sit still? Just listen? This was a new concept for me, so I continued to probe her heart for exactly what she meant. My struggle was obvious, yet she kept pointing me back to listening with my heart.

Since our time on the porch I'm still learning to be still and listen with my heart to the voice of God. I'm a little wiser in that I lean in a little closer to hear the heart of the one sharing but not wise enough to practice this art of selflessness faithfully. I continue to ask the Lord to help me take the time to lean in as I listen to him and to others.

Boundaries

Just imagine a child with no boundaries and how reckless, self-centered, and out of control that little person would grow up to become. That's what a mentoring relationship without boundaries is like—chaotic! We all need boundaries in our relationships; otherwise we begin to feel taken advantage of, unappreciated, and completely spent, as though we can give no more!

When formally establishing a mentoring relationship, it's important that both women agree to things such as what's appropriate at work, what's open for discussion, expectations of the relationship, time involvement, or a number of other considerations.

When I first started mentoring a young woman at my job, it was very informal; nonetheless I made some mental notes for our relationship but especially for my behavior. I was her supervisor and felt it necessary to take extra measures to ensure that I was not being manipulative, overly demanding, or intrusive with her personal life.

I desired to encourage Karen both professionally and spiritually. Of utmost importance was conveying my availability to her and that I was in her corner. We made it clear that we respected one another's time, space, privacy, and confidentiality, which gave us greater room to be open and honest. The boundaries were not bogging us down but providing safety and freedom in our relationship.

What is appropriate for one mentoring relationship to succeed may be the very thing impeding another. Just because I like to talk about everything doesn't mean she does or has to. I may think getting together every couple of weeks for lunch is great; she may feel that once a month is enough and lunch is not necessary. When considering the many variables, we need to consider each woman's personality, desire, and interest in forming this special relationship.

Boundaries based on personal preferences provide freedom. Boundaries based on other things, such as control, fear, or selfishness, become bondage. Just as God has established boundaries for coming to him (through his Son), we need boundaries that enhance our relationships and draw us together. Pray that your mentoring relationships are freed, not bound, by boundaries.

Resources

I've never known a spiritually or professionally dedicated woman who didn't welcome new information. Titus 3:13–14 tells us we are to help others learn to do good and lead a productive life. Sharing information is one way we can accomplish this.

If we are to remain on the cutting edge professionally, we need to share work-related information. Early in my career I was encouraged to become familiar with all aspects of human resources, which involved joining professional and management organizations, attending workshops, getting acquainted with others in the field, and subscribing to a slew of published resources. These resources benefited me in subsequent career opportunities, especially as I acquired new responsibilities.

Just as these basics hold true professionally, so it is in spiritual mentoring. Many women are struggling with workplace issues and need to be directed to other resources to encourage them throughout the day. The best starting place is passages of the Bible specific to the situation. However, we can't stop there. God has given us a great number of other spiritual resources including books by Christian authors, tapes, conferences, church programs, and other Christian people.

Resources are good tools and become invaluable when shared at the right time with the right person. Who knows? Information you provide may be the key that opens the door to a new career opportunity or spiritual truth. Pray for ways to learn from the Lord what the best resource available is and for ways to share what you have already learned on your journey with others.

Friendships of Value

First Thessalonians 5:11 says, "Therefore encourage one another and build each other up, just as in fact you are doing."

If only we would do this more, how different our workplaces and lives would be.

Up until this point we've thought about our ministry to others in the workplace. But now let's shift our thinking and talk specifically about our role and responsibility with other believers in the workplace.

As sisters in Christ we are to be in harmony with one another, take responsibility for one another, and experience the joy that comes from being united in the same family, or, as Colossians 2:2 says, "be encouraged in heart and united in love."

The apostle Paul wrote these words to the believers at Colosse. It's presumed he had never actually been to the church or met the believers, but because he loved his family (other believers), his heart was burdened for them. He yearned for them to continue in their belief of Christ's teachings and to draw strength from one another. I can't compare myself to Paul, but I can tell you that my heart's desire is that we become as *soul sisters*.

When Paul uses the phrase "encouraged in heart and united in love," he desires that believers be woven so closely together in their affection and love for one another that they can encourage one another at the core of their thoughts and feelings. I believe this passage admonishes us to not take lightly the fellowship that flows from our relationship with Christ, to have the same purposefulness concerning Christ, to love abundantly, to esteem others greatly, and to celebrate continuously Christ in our life.

As Christian women we should get excited when we meet or hear about another "family member" in the workplace. Not so we can hang out with one another or so we can snub others but because we have two invaluable gifts in common: Jesus Christ residing in our hearts and eternal life. Finding out that my girlfriend Tracey and I were going to be experiencing pregnancy at the same time was cause for a celebration. Despite the fact that she lived in Georgia and I lived in Kansas, we felt more closely connected to one another because of this precious bond. When we talked about the challenges of weight gain or the blessings of baby movements, we were encouraging one another in heart and being united in love.

Appreciate the friendships God has placed in your life. The Christian woman you are overlooking in your workplace may be the very person who will intercede for you on your job, be your codefender of the faith, help you up when you feel like staying down, or stand by you when you feel you are walking alone. Pray that the Lord will help you see how good and pleasant it is—like precious oil—when we live together in unity (Ps. 133:1).

• • •

Personal Insight

What new truths has God revealed to you? How will you depend on the Holy Spirit so you can be a messenger of God's truth to others around you? _____

_____

_____

_____

• • •

Spiritual Application

Write out the Scripture verse(s) in this chapter that gave you encouragement for your current work situation. _____

_____

_____

_____

How is God speaking to you through this verse?_____

_____

_____

_____

What workplace actions will you commit to following through on as you strive to fulfill God's purpose for you in the workplace? _____

_____

_____

_____

7

Intended to Harm

Discrimination
and Harassment at Work

You intended to harm me, but God intended it for good.

Genesis 50:20

In my anguish I cried to the LORD, and he answered by set-
ting me free. The LORD is with me; I will not be afraid. What
can man do to me? The LORD is with me; he is my helper. I
will look in triumph on my enemies.

Psalm 118:5–7

Most women I know either have been or know someone who has been affected by unfair employment
practices or harassment because of race, religion,
age, or gender. Personally, I've been subjected to these ills
within the workplace and have grappled with trusting God,
walking in peace, and experiencing victory in these unbeliev-

ably difficult situations. Therefore this chapter is not so much about a "human resources approach" to combating discrimination or harassment in the workplace as it is about spiritually and personally triumphing over adverse circumstances because of Jesus Christ in your life.

Fighting against discrimination or harassment is no small feat. It is often an out-and-out war. If there's ever a time for believers to pray for, encourage, and uplift another believer, this is such a time, as we see in the story of the Israelites fighting against the Amalekites (Exod. 17:8–16).

Doom seemed imminent in face of the fierce enemy, the Amalekites, but in this amazing story of the weak overcoming the strong, we see God demonstrate the strength of believers coming together in his name to win a war against the enemy.

The Amalekites were the first group of people to lead an attack against the Israelites after they fled Egypt. The Amalekites were a treacherously fierce and powerful tribe, known for brutal attacks and plundering weaker campsites for personal and selfish gain. True to reputation, they attacked the Israelites. In defense, Moses instructed Joshua to prepare for battle against their adversaries.

While Joshua prepared for war, Moses declared, "Tomorrow I will stand on top of the hill with the staff of God in my hands" (v. 9). Moses knew the only way the Israelites could overcome the Amalekites was through God's divine intervention and help. Therefore his statement gives reverence to God's power and also encouragement to Joshua. I imagine Joshua drew great strength and resolve as he saw Moses "cheering" him on with hands uplifted to God.

When the battle began, "As long as Moses held up his hands, the Israelites were winning, but whenever he lowered his hands, the Amalekites were winning. . . . Aaron and Hur held his hands up—one on one side, one on the other" (vv. 11–12). Not only does this passage demonstrate the importance of our spiritual role in interceding for other believers but also the practical demands that may be required to help.

In this story Moses encouraged Joshua by leaning on God's power and being a vehicle of prayer. Aaron and Hur encouraged Moses by lending physical and undoubtedly spiritual support. The end result? The Amalekites were defeated. God could have moved independently of all of these men but instead chose to use those who were serving him and united in purpose so he could be glorified.

Those fighting on both sides of that war knew the one true God was being exalted and lifted up high. Similarly, we need to demonstrate the power of unity as we stand together in prayer, in encouragement, and in God's truth to do battle with the "Amalekite" in our workplace.

Together the Israelites experienced God as their banner of protection and were given a glimpse of the character of *Jehovah-nissi,* "The Lord My Banner." As we stand united in the Lord and face the enemy, we too can experience God's hand of protection.

Even if you don't have a Moses- or Aaron-like friend standing in the gap for you, know that God is upholding you always. Isaiah 41:10 says, "Do not fear, for I am with you; do not be dismayed, for I am your God. I will strengthen you and help you; I will uphold you with my righteous right hand."

Enduring Discrimination and Harassment

Christ knows about unjust discrimination and harassment firsthand. When we consider unjust employment practices, we must be mindful that Christ gave up his rightful title of

God to become man. He was demoted from king to carpenter and from saint to "sinner" (the one bearing our sins) so that we could be given eternal life. He had his office moved from streets of gold to roads of dust. And then he exceeded his job description by washing feet, sitting with lepers, talking with beggars, and being a servant to everyone he met. And this is only the beginning.

In John chapters 18 and 19, we read of incomprehensible harassment as he is falsely accused, bitterly betrayed, spat upon, slapped, flogged, whipped, crowned with thorns, viciously mocked, stripped, and crucified on a cross like a common criminal. I can't even imagine the outcry if someone had to endure this sort of treatment today in America—yet this happened to our Lord and Savior.

Our Savior endured racial, ethnic, religious, and other forms of bigotry, especially from those professing to be upholding the law. I don't think it's a stretch at all to say that our Lord and Savior knows what you and I feel when discrimination or harassment happens to us. In fact, Hebrews 4:15 tells us he is able to sympathize with us.

Yes, Jesus knows precisely what it is like to be unjustly discriminated against and brutally harassed. Suffering and enduring the pain of man's attack is something our Savior is all too familiar with. And despite man's attempt to strip Christ of his sovereignty by placing his personal worth at thirty silver coins, his story didn't end with man's judgment and neither should yours.

As Christian women in the workplace, our story of discrimination or harassment must start and end with God's truth, "You intended to harm me, but God intended it for good" (Gen. 50:20). Overcoming discrimination and harassment in the workplace is about God's truth being poured into your life so that others can see the power of Jesus in you. He is our example because he trampled the unjust circumstances of discrimination and harassment under his foot, and so can you with him by your side.

I believe you want to experience God's truth in your life, so let's delve right into what I believe God has given us to triumph over the enemies of discrimination and harassment in the workplace.

Discrimination and Harassment in the Workplace

Although I will address both discrimination and harassment in the same breath, I believe them to be two different beasts feeding off of the same poison of stereotypes, ignorance, assumptions, and self-exalted pride. At the core of each is the need to strip a person of her value (personal and professional) in the workplace, usually exhibited through an attitude, action, or approach.

To better help you understand what I mean, consider these work-related situations.

Work Situation One: A director finds out that a newly hired male is being compensated more than she is despite his inexperience and the fact that she's training him. A salary analysis indicates a large disparity among female and male directors within the company, but correcting it would be too costly so nothing is done.

Work Situation Two: Two female employees apply for a vacant administrative position in the company. Although Employee B is more skilled for the job, Employee A receives the promotion because her aunt, who is well connected within the company, knows the director with the vacant administrative position.

Work Situation Three: A research associate begins feeling uncomfortable with her male supervisor, who inappropriately stares at her upper body during conversations. She tries to avoid her supervisor at all costs, but given the confines of the department, it's virtually impossible.

Work Situation Four: A female employee begins receiving gifts and love notes in the office mail from a male coworker. She makes it clear that their relationship is strictly professional. The male coworker responds by sending a letter of apology and another gift to her home.

In each of the above workplace situations, the individual's personal and professional value was compromised and violated. Whether a subtle act of discrimination or an overt action of harassment, these types of situations do happen in the workplace. As believers we need to have a spiritual defense against those who would seek to strip us of our value. But before we look at how to spiritually and personally overcome these obstacles, let me briefly share with you what I believe discrimination and harassment are *not* so you don't become deceived by misdirection, the enemy's lies, or other people's agendas.

Discrimination and harassment are real forces to be reckoned with; however, not all attitudes, actions, or statements should be lumped under these categories. Therefore as a believer you need to be very careful not to stamp someone with a "scarlet letter." Attaching accusing words to another person in the workplace too loosely, quickly, or flippantly can be devastating for all concerned. Once marked, the person will find it nearly impossible to remove the stain. Let me give you an example.

With a list of complaints in her hand, a female employee made some startling allegations against her male supervisor. She presented her case with conviction and assurance, giving me detailed accounts of work situations that supported her accusations. At the end of our meeting, I telephoned her supervisor, who immediately came down to my office.

Shortly into our conversation the supervisor revealed various work situations in which the employee was disrespectful, insubordinate to his authority, and verbally abusive to him and other coworkers.

I quickly saw that this was not a case of discrimination or harassment but of an employee shirking her personal and professional responsibilities in the workplace. Her careless and vindictive words took less than one hour to air but took the company close to six months to repair.

I learned long ago that not everyone who cries "Wolf!" is being attacked—but they may very well be the wolf in sheep's clothing. Many women are not being rightfully promoted, compensated, or esteemed as valuable professionals in the workplace, and this can be very upsetting. But filing a claim of discrimination or harassment is serious business and must never be used to get your way, be vindictive, or try to achieve monetary gain.

Psalm 43:3 says, "Send forth your light and your truth, let them guide me." I encourage you to pray this prayer as you seek answers about what you should do and how to proceed in the case of discrimination or harassment. Otherwise, disregarding truth can turn you into the very thing you despise in those who seek to strip you of your value in the workplace.

Overcoming Discrimination and Harassment in the Workplace

Every professional bone in me believes in seeking the advice of a good human resources professional, adhering to company policies and procedures, and possibly attending to the counsel of legal advisors to handle discrimination and harassment.

At the same time, every spiritual bone in my body knows that the only way to experience personal peace and spiritual victory over your situation, regardless of the outcome, is with scriptural truth.

Jeremiah 17:5 says, "Cursed is the one who trusts in man, who depends on flesh for his strength and whose heart turns away from the LORD." Do you consider yourself so self-sufficient and self-determined that you often turn away from God's truth and do it your way? Well, I have tried this! And when I did, I was in essence turning my back on God, just as you in fact are doing when you "take matters into your own hands."

Plenty of times in my career I've witnessed the mistreatment of others in the workplace. And just as often I've attempted to rectify the situation by advocating for that rightful salary increase, promotion, or recognition. Sometimes I was successful in my petitions, yet other times I felt my efforts were in vain. During these latter times I sometimes felt like quitting or giving up.

In my heart I knew that this sense of despair usually came over me in direct correlation to my shift of trust from God to myself or others. Hopelessness is one of the curses that comes from ungoverned trust in man and self. So I caution you, if you are fighting this war against discrimination or harassment in the workplace and feeling hopeless, you have stopped trusting in God. Most likely you've done as I have done in the past, which is to stake too much of your hope in the decision, in the system working, or in others doing the right thing, instead of in God.

Our hope must be placed in the Lord. "But blessed is the man who trusts in the LORD, whose confidence is in him. He will be like a tree planted by the water. . . . It does not fear . . . its leaves are always green . . . It has no worries . . . and never fails to bear fruit" (Jer. 17:7–8). When our hope is in the Lord, we receive blessings that include being strengthened, satisfied, courageous, and fruitful. God's blessings enable you to endure with confidence and walk in victory through unbelievably backbreaking, knee-bending times in the workplace because the Keeper of Hope is holding you.

No matter what has happened to you or is happening right now, as you seize God's truth and let it take over, you will experience firsthand what it means to be more than a conqueror over the circumstances of discrimination and harassment. The truth is that God desires for you to look to him and not at your circumstances.

Along with trust in God, four "truths" can help us spiritually and personally overcome the beasts of discrimination and harassment in the workplace: *remember truth, report truth, rest in truth, and reconcile truth.* God's tools in your hands can equip you to triumph over your workplace struggles. I pray that by the time you finish this chapter you'll be proactive in living out these four truths for experiencing victory in the workplace every day.

Remember Truth

Jesus tells us in John 17:17 that God's words are truth. The first step to overcoming this adversity in the workplace is to *remember truth.* God is truth, and he upholds truth even when lies, schemes, and deceit appear to be prevailing against you. As Christians we must cling to God's truth because our very existence depends on it. Once God's truth is embedded in our hearts, minds, and souls, remembering it will become second nature. Nothing, including harassment, will be able to shake us loose from remembering it.

The one truth that is essential in relation to discrimination and harassment in the workplace is Hebrews 4:13: "Nothing in all creation is hidden from God's sight. Everything is uncovered and laid bare before the eyes of him to whom we must give account."

The devil will try to deceive you into believing that those in your workplace who scheme and plot are getting away with something or doing something in secret. But God's truth is this: Not one thing can escape him. Even the schemes done in utter darkness by your adversaries lie exposed before God.

In the Old Testament we see a case of discrimination and harassment in the third chapter of the Book of Esther. Haman, a descendant of the Amalekites (whom we discussed earlier), is second in command to King Xerxes. For all intents and purposes, Haman has the world in his hands. However, because of pride, arrogance, and self-importance, he harbors hatred in his heart against the Jews and becomes enraged when a Jewish man named Mordecai refuses to bow down before him.

Like most folks who have "issues," Haman's hatred feeds on his pride and fuels his prejudices. But unlike most people, he secretly schemes and plots the widespread genocide of God's people—all because the seed of hatred has taken root. Esther 3:6 states, "Yet having learned who Mordecai's people were, he scorned the idea of killing only Mordecai. Instead Haman looked for a way to destroy all Mordecai's people, the Jews." Talk about feeding the beast of discrimination and harassment with stereotypes, assumptions, ignorance, and self-exalted pride. This is it!

As the story unfolds we see God's righteous hand of protection and judgment move in miraculous and unforeseen ways. Haman is hung from the very gallows he had built earlier to hang Mordecai; the Jewish people are delivered from the hatred, discrimination, and harassment; and Mordecai reigns as second in command to King Xerxes, the same position previously held by Haman.

God is truth and all will have to give account to him (1 Peter 4:5) regardless of their power, position, and prejudices. If or when you go through the difficult times of discrimination and harassment in the workplace, remember, God is upholding truth.

Mordecai knew God personally, as we see in his refusal to bow down before Haman and acknowledge him as "a god." Therefore committing to God's truth was embedded in Mordecai's heart *before* he was tested. As a result, remembering truth was first nature to him even while staring persecution and death in the face. Similarly, as a Christian woman, the only way to remember God's truth is to experience him. Hide his truth in your heart as you meditate on it, study it, and live it out for yourself *now!*

If you don't commit anything else to memory, know his truth is worth remembering! Only one question remains: Is your knowledge of God's truth so implanted in your life that nothing can uproot it from your heart—including what you are currently facing?

Report the Truth

We've all heard, "Do you swear to tell the truth, the whole truth, and nothing but the truth?" As Christian women it's critical that we speak truthfully and do not intentionally slander one another with our words (Ps. 15:2–3).

Once words are spoken they become powerful instruments for either God's purposes or the devil's purposes. Intentionally exaggerating even a little bit or deliberately omitting "insignificant" details to make your case sound more convincing will malign your character, ruin your Christian witness, and impact your fellowship with God.

Those besieging you base their actions on lies and deception; therefore you must stay clear of this path at all costs in your lifestyle, spoken words, and written documentation. All three are powerful weapons when it comes to refuting or representing one's case. Because we've talked about the importance of your lifestyle and words in previous chapters, let's focus here on something rarely discussed: reporting the truth through written documentation.

The Bible is a great example of documentation. Let's revisit the story of the Israelites defeating the Amalekites in Exodus 17. At the end of this battle God tells Moses to "write this on a scroll as something to be remembered" because he plans to blot out the memory of the Amalekites from history (Exod. 17:14).

If you want to see firsthand a good example of reporting truth through good documentation, I encourage you to read Exodus 17:8–16. Moses' account of this war includes four essentials to documentation: *who* (Amalekites, Joshua, Aaron, Hur, God, and Moses himself), *what* (initial attack, defense, and victory), *when* (time frame of situation and following events), and *where* (top of the hill, altar).

This is the goal of documentation: to report truth that concentrates on facts such as the who, what, when, and where of your overall situation. Moses writes all this *and* summarizes it in five paragraphs (in the NIV translation). Now that's what I would call reporting truth with good documentation!

If we weren't living in such a litigious environment, these guidelines would be enough. However, to be safe let me add five more basics to documentation that you should consider for your workplace:

1. Keep documentation separate from your personal and planning calendar (otherwise personal or private notes may become public information).

2. Write your notes in ink using a bound notepad (pages and words are less likely to be changed without your knowledge).

3. Check your employee manual or handbook for documentation guidance (or consult with human resources, especially when supervising others).

4. Ensure confidentiality by securing the information in a locked drawer.

5. Report truth professionally and objectively (this is not a venting tool or diary).

Documentation is a good instrument for reporting work-related situations that increase or decrease your value in the workplace. However, like anything else, when used to slander someone, to repeat the grapevine news, or for office gossip, it becomes a tool for the enemy. Remember, reporting truth isn't about writing down every conversation, look, or innuendo. It's not about policing others' actions, words, or behaviors. Nor is it something you spend thirty minutes a day or week writing down. And most importantly, it's not a trump card you broadcast to the world.

Truthful and concise documentation should help you, the human resources department, and anyone making a decision on your behalf. Documentation is not an end all; it's only one of many professional instruments at your disposal. Without a doubt, the greatest truth you will ever report comes from living out God's Word in your workplace. In and out of the workplace, "I urge you to live a life worthy of the calling you have received" (Eph. 4:1). This is documentation everyone can see without you even writing a word.

Rest in Truth

Matthew 11:28 says, "Come to me, all you who are weary and burdened, and I will give you rest." Since Jesus said it, you can count on the fact that the devil will try to snatch it, distort it, defile it, and do everything else possible to hinder you from attaining what Jesus has purposed for you—rest!

In Greek, the rest Jesus promises means "inward tranquility while one performs necessary labor."[1] Yet for many women in the workplace, enduring the day-to-day pains inherent in discrimination and harassment makes it hard to hold onto God's promises or imagine experiencing "inner tranquility." But this is what the Lord promises for believers: inner joy, peace, love, and all other blessings that come from his truth.

God's truth is the only way to experience victory over discrimination or harassment in the workplace. If we are to rest in these spiritual promises and experience victory over our oppressors, we must hand over worry for his peace, bitterness for his forgiveness, chaos for his serenity, despair for his hope, independence for his dependence, and most importantly, deception for his truth.

Jeremiah 15:16 says, "When your words came, I ate them; they were my joy and my heart's delight." When I think of Jeremiah's words, my mind races to a bakery window adorned with fresh strawberry cheesecake, chocolate mousse soufflé, raisin scones drizzled with icing, and everything else made of sugar. Just as it's natural for me to sit here and think about what those goodies will taste like, so God wants us to dwell on his words. He wants us to feast at his banquet table (called the Word) and feed off of it to our heart's delight.

Unlike with desserts, when we partake of his words, we don't have to worry about the fat grams or calories. Its richness is manifested in the rest we experience, especially during our times of testing, trials, and difficulty. As author Francis Frangipane says, "To enter God's rest requires we abide in full surrender to His will, in perfect trust of His power. To rest from our labors does not mean we have stopped working; it means we have stopped the laborious work of the flesh. It means we have entered the eternal works which He brings forth through us."[2]

God is able to do exceedingly more than we can ever imagine, and that includes giving us rest in the throes of our circumstances. His rest is just the beginning of his power manifested in your life. However, in order for you to experience his promise of rest, you must take him at his word. You must know that every time you seek him, you'll find him. Every time you abide in him, you'll experience him. Every time you obey him, you'll receive him. Without fail, every time you trust him, you'll rest in him. In essence, knowing him is rest and to rest is to know him.

The only truth I know rests on Jesus' words, "My yoke is easy and my burden is light" (Matt. 11:30). The challenge remains: Will you know his rest during your difficult times?

Reconcile Truth

Did you know that our Savior prayed to our heavenly Father for you and me? Shortly before being betrayed into the hands of his enemies, Jesus prayed to the Holy Father on our behalf, "My prayer is not that you take them out of the world but that you protect them from the evil one. . . . Sanctify them by the truth; your word is truth" (John 17:15–17).

In ways you and I will never fathom, Jesus communing with the Father about our well-being is like having all the great spiritual giants like Abraham, Moses, Joshua, Esther, Mary,

Paul, and John assemble together and beseech God on our behalf—only a bazillion times more powerful!

Recently, my childhood girlfriend called me for prayer. After we prayed she said, "I feel so much better knowing you are praying for me." Reflecting on her words put Jesus' prayer in perspective for me. If God allowed her to experience comfort from my words, what does he anticipate our response to Jesus' words will be? Just stop for a moment and meditate on the thought of Jesus praying for you!

I don't know about you, but I'm sitting here shouting like a crazy woman, "Hallelujah, praise your holy name!" I can't imagine resting in a greater truth than knowing *the* great prayer warrior, Jesus, has interceded and still is interceding on my behalf. Wow!

Once you reconcile this truth—you accept God's divine favor—in your life, you will never be the same. And guess what? There's more! Catch this vision with me: Jesus, fully God and fully human (Matt. 1:20–23), knew of the inhumane discrimination and harassment that lay before him, yet because of his lavish love for us sought the Father on our behalf and prayed specifically for protection and provision—protection from the evil one and provision to be sanctified (or made holy, set apart to do his will) by the Word of truth.

Instead of praying for a way of escape from his trials and temptations, as I'm certain I would have, Jesus demonstrated an outpouring of immeasurable, unadulterated love toward us and reconciled our spiritual well-being to the Father. Talk about discovering a pot of gold! On the one hand it's incomprehensible that Jesus prays for you and me, and on the other it's exhilarating because our lives are crowned with God's protection and the Holy Spirit's provision.

How fabulous is that? Jesus could have prayed that we'd be protected from the suffering, pain, and heartache around us, but instead he prayed "to give them such grace that they may endure all trials and be sustained amid them."[3] We have divine protection from the enemy and provision to do God's will so that when everything is said and done, God is glorified.

As contrary as it is to our natural disposition, we need to undergo testing and trials so that we can unconditionally experience God's power, strength, and truth. Jesus experienced this truth as he endured persecution, discrimination, and the cross in order for the Father to be glorified (John 17:1). Recognizing Jesus as the ultimate example, we too must endure so both the Father and Son are glorified!

Because of Jesus' life, death, and resurrection, we are now reconciled to the Father and "are therefore Christ's ambassadors" (2 Cor. 5:18–20). As we act on Christ's behalf we must make his truth in our lives evident through obedience. We can't just say we believe God's Word; we must obey God's Word. Obedience requires accepting God's divine truth *and* then living it out.

This is a spiritual decision that each of us must make daily, especially when we are compelled by our sinful, fearful nature to do otherwise. Reconciling ourselves to God's truth means laying aside our "rightful" indignation, professional outrage, and self-centered pride to completely and thoroughly experience the author of truth himself. It's laying aside our inability for his ability. And it's unwaveringly living out his truths because *he* is able!

Enduring hardships is costly and none are exempt from it, yet as we reconcile God's truth in our lives, we come to experience him personally and intimately. In all situations when it appeared that discrimination or harassment won out, we know otherwise. Scripture shows us that Moses wrote about his victory, Mordecai lived out his victory, and Jesus became our victory. The God we serve is *truth* and declares that it is he who gives strength to his people (Ps. 29:11).

Let's thank the Lord that we are reconciled through his Son and reconcile his truth in our lives so that he may be glorified. I pray that he will surpass our expectations as we remember his truth, report the truth, rest in the truth, and become reconciled to his truth.

• • •

Personal Insight

What new truths has God revealed to you? How will you depend on the Holy Spirit so discrimination or harassment doesn't devour your internal hope and joy in the Lord? _____

_____

_____

_____

_____

• • •

Spiritual Application

Write out the Scripture verse(s) in this chapter that gave you encouragement for your current work situation. _____

_____

_____

_____

_____

How is God speaking to you through this verse? _____

_____

_____

_____

What workplace actions will you commit to following through on as you reconcile God's truth in your life? _____

_____

_____

_____

8

A New Thing!

Seeking God before Job Searching

See, I am doing a new thing! Now it springs up; do you not perceive it? I am making a way in the desert and streams in the wasteland.

Isaiah 43:19

"That's it! I quit!" This is how my first real job ended. I was working at a fast-food restaurant during college and in the middle of "May I take your order?" a construction worker verbally assaulted me with a tirade of inappropriate remarks. Minutes later I was out the door, never to return . . . except to get my last paycheck . . . oh, and to get a meal occasionally!

Have you ever been so exasperated by someone or something at your job that you felt like quitting? We often feel that way in direct relationship to a heightened work situation that seemingly pushes us over the edge. Once we are pushed to this breaking point, we begin our job search, even if just in our minds.

Although I wouldn't surrender that much control to someone else now, at eighteen life seemed fragile enough to justify my decision to quit. And back then I didn't recognize that my paycheck was from a business entity and my working was for the Lord (John 9:4). Acknowledging this truth now puts my work commitment into perspective and sends me searching for God's will *before* searching for a new job.

Seeking God First

Changing jobs without seeking the Lord's will is like saying, "I know I work for you, but I make the final decisions about when to stay and when to leave." Would you ever take a trip to a new city at night, without directions, by yourself . . . knowing your car lights weren't working? Yet this is what we do when we don't seek God first.

When David penned the words, "Your word is a lamp to my feet and a light for my path" (Ps. 119:105), he did so as a means of praise and in recognition of the awesome power and wisdom found in following God's precepts. He fully understood that it was only God's Word that gave him wisdom, insight, and strength to live each day.

Recently a friend sought my advice about moving to another state for career advancement opportunities. Everything sounded good, and in the world's eyes it was the "opportunity of a lifetime." Most people would have jumped at the opportunity without hesitation. Yet my friend wrestled with her decision. She desired God's will and didn't want to be persuaded by the world's idea of success or personal ambitions.

After weeks of praying with her and discussing the spiritual, professional, and emotional implications of such a move, I felt led to write down some questions for her consideration. The following questions are slightly different, but the idea of seeking God remains the same. Proverbs 16:9 says, "In his heart a man plans his course, but the LORD determines his steps." In light of this verse, take a moment to consider what it means to seek God's will before making that next career move by answering these questions:

1. What is God's specific purpose for you at your workplace right now? If you are uncertain, take time to reflect on what he's been showing you in your quiet time and through prayer.

2. Have you determined to live out that purpose in your workplace? Explain how you have or why you have not.

3. What areas do you feel God is refining in your life right now before placing you in a new position or place of employment? Are you willing to join in with him during this refinement time?

4. If God says, "Not now, stay!" or "Get ready, go!" will you be able to praise him with a joyful heart? Why or why not?

5. Will you commit your plans to his will? If yes, how? If not, why not?

Some of these questions may seem difficult to answer, yet we must come face-to-face with our heartfelt answers if we are truly seeking God's will.

Having a list of pros and cons is good, but we must use the light, God's Word, to direct our paths and give us perspective. His voice must be the authoritative voice behind all our decisions. He is our primary source of guidance. Let us trust in him with all our heart and lean not on our own understanding but in all our ways acknowledge him so he can make our paths straight (Prov. 3:5–6).

If seeking the Lord seems undesirable to you, then recognize that you will reap consequences. For "anyone, then, who knows the good he ought to do and doesn't do it, sins" (James 4:17). Knowing what God's Word tells us to do and deciding against it is rebellion and leads to broken fellowship with him. I can recall a period of time when I had no sense of direction or purpose in life. Everything I did seemed pointless. Absolutely everything seemed senseless and painstakingly exhausting!

It wasn't until I came face-to-face with my rebellious, independent spirit that I realized that my ears were opened to God but my heart shut off to obeying him. I was living in direct disobedience to God's Word and knew it! Whenever we willfully transgress against God's truths and don't seek repentance, our fellowship with him is violated. Think back to a time when a friend or family member hurt you and then tried to carry on a "heart-to-heart" conversation as though nothing happened. Didn't you feel the strain, loss of intimacy, and distance? How much more is this magnified when we have unconfessed sin and attempt to come before our holy Father without a repentant heart?

God deplores sin; therefore, until we obey his Word and seek forgiveness, we are unable to clearly hear him and enjoy the fellowship Jesus died to give us. We know why we feel isolated and all alone because 2 Chronicles 15:2 says, "The LORD is with you when you are with him. If you seek him, he will be found by you, but if you forsake him, he will forsake you."

When I consider my life in the workplace during that time I was living in disobedience, I know it didn't mirror a life for Christ but one of self. Had someone taken inventory of my lifestyle or commitments, they would have seen the same worldly cravings of someone searching for the earthly pleasures of status, social standing, and lots of stuff. I distinctly remember this period in my life as one of perpetual job searching.

An incident that readily comes to mind is when all my efforts to land "the" job engulfed me like an ocean wave. A senior director recommended me to her friend for an exciting management position in downtown Washington, D.C. I'm a city girl at heart, so this was an added bonus. No doubt about it, this job had my name on it—no need for anyone else to pursue it. Right?

As I became so self-focused on landing the perfect job, my eyes grew wider, my goals loftier, and God's light dimmer. I felt suffocated in my current position, which made it easier in my mind to justify not trusting God. "After all," I rationalized, "why would God keep me in such a predicament anyway?"

In the process of trying to get this job, I lied to my boss to schedule my interview, fudged numbers to increase my current salary, and had a terrible interview. No one would have ever imagined that I made a living in human resources management. I did just about everything I had advised others against doing.

Ugh! Things couldn't have felt worse; however, I had dug my own hole. Even if I got the position (I didn't), there was no way that I could give God any glory. The whole process was a farce. Had I sought the Lord about my decision to proceed, who knows, maybe I would have landed the job of a lifetime.

As unsettling as it may sound to those of you who just can't wait to "get out," seeking God before searching affirms that you really desire God's best for your life. If you did not answer the questions earlier in this chapter, I encourage you to go back to them now. God has great plans for your life. Your efforts will not be in vain but be fruitful and pleasing to him as you prepare for the new things he has in store for you at your current position and elsewhere.

Preparing for a New Thing!

With the exception of my short-lived stint as one of the hundred "sweatshop queens" at a film processing factory, I have always taken significantly longer to find the right job than most employment books indicate it should take. After six months of diligently looking, it's easy to become discouraged when you receive yet another rejection letter, wade through the Sunday paper, or tell people at church, "No, I'm still looking!" for the umpteenth time. Whether you find employment sooner or later than expected, the key is to be prepared for your search and whatever "new thing" God has in store for you.

As you embrace God's plan, your journey will be that much more successful. As Christian women you have all the knowledge, skills, and abilities necessary to complete his job assignment—and that includes job hunting.

In the performance workshops I used to conduct, I would often refer to the knowledge, skills, and abilities (also known as KSAs) of the employee. These three components are considered essential to employee performance. For years I thought they were identified by a human resources guru or consultant, so imagine my surprise when I read about them in the Old Testament. I just about fell out of my chair!

KSAs in the Old Testament? I could hardly believe what I was reading, but there it was in black and white. Exodus 31:3 tells us that God filled the craftsmen working on the tabernacle with knowledge, skills, and abilities to accomplish his will. Won't the human resources gurus be surprised when they realize they didn't really come up with this concept? I smile at this because so often we think we've created something, failing to realize that only the Creator creates—we merely copy!

Discovering that KSAs are in the Bible confirmed my belief in the importance of being prepared. Employers want to know that they are hiring or promoting knowledgeable, skilled, and able professionals who bring useful and profitable attributes to the company. Therefore if you desire to work in management, you should take a leadership course and seek other ways to improve your KSAs. The same principle holds true for any job or career change. Landing a job or embarking on a new career opportunity will require keeping abreast of the evolving profession or trade you are in or desire to be in. Essentially, the more knowledge you have, the more marketable you become and the greater your career choices are. The more refined your skills and abilities, the greater your opportunities for getting hired or promoted. Preparation can only lead to new things.

God is faithfully looking out for you, guaranteed. As we stand on God's truth, he will open the doors we are to walk through and close the ones we are not to go through. Sounds like a plan! Now the question to you is, "How committed are you to receiving what God has prepared for you once you realize that job hunting is labor?" Yes, it's fruitful labor but labor nonetheless.

Even when you know God has given you the green light, job hunting is like running a race . . . a long marathon! The reality is that you have to pace yourself. I'd be lying to you if I gave you the impression that looking for a job was simply a matter of reading your Bible and praying. These are a must; however, you must commit to some additional aspects of preparation if you desire to take hold of the job God has for you.

The job market is highly competitive. I say that not to discourage you but to let you know that finding a job may be more difficult than you think, but with God it is not impossible. Nothing is beyond your grasp as you seek him first. Confident that his will is your desire because you expect the best, let's look at the key element to preparing for a successful job search: being proactive!

Being a Proactive Candidate

Webster's defines *proactive* as "before the current process of change."[1] In the human resources field we use this word to indicate the innovation of a person, product, or idea. In this sense being proactive is a personal principle that sets you apart as a person of excellence striving to accomplish God's purpose.

In order to be a proactive job seeker, you must be a person who recognizes the importance of being these seven things: professional, diligent, prompt, organized, committed, considerate, and exceptional.

HR Tip #1: Be Professional

A proactive person is professional! You can have the best intentions in the world, but if you don't come across as polished, you'll undermine what you are attempting to accomplish. The way your resume looks, how you answer a business call, and your interviewing mannerisms all will affect how others perceive you.

Having done my share of recruitment and interviewing, I found that professionalism is the area lacking in most candidates. I cannot count how many candidates never made it past the telephone screening process or were never called back for a follow-up interview because of a lack of basic professional and business etiquette.

Candidates have sent resumes and cover letters laden with misspellings and typos. They have called me by the wrong name, mispronounced the name of the company, or forgotten which position they had applied for. One female candidate's safety pin came unfastened and her suit jacket popped open, exposing her undergarment and bare skin. Had she taken more time to consider her professional attire, she would have worn a blouse under her suit jacket. Don't make any of these mistakes!

Scriptural Encouragement: "In everything set them an example by doing what is good . . . so that those who oppose you may be ashamed because they have nothing bad to say about us" (Titus 2:7–8).

HR Tip #2: Be Diligent

A proactive person is diligent! You don't have to start your job hunt in fifth gear, but try to maintain a consistent pace that keeps you on top of your search throughout the race. Remember, the process of transitioning from one job to another often takes longer than expected. Continue to be diligent, turning over every stone, especially after the six-month lull you will feel.

The Sunday paper is a great resource for job hunting; however, it's only one of many resources available. Consider the various business and trade journals or professional magazines that include an employment section at the end of each publication. You can also check the midweek business section of your local paper and a plethora of job web sites. If you feel comfortable with employment and recruiting firms, this could also be another avenue to pursue. Just be aware of any out-of-pocket expenses.

Scriptural Encouragement: "The plans of the diligent lead to profit" (Prov. 21:5).

HR Tip #3: Be Prompt

A proactive person is prompt! Once you discover all the possible business opportunities to research, you must recognize the importance of being prompt. When something piques your interest even slightly, it's to your advantage to respond as quickly as possible.

Ask anyone working in recruitment and they will tell you that once a job announcement appears, their in-boxes are instantly inundated with resumes. While I was job hunting my goal was to submit my cover letter and resume to the appropriate person that same day or the next at the latest. I set aside time during the weekend and midweek just to job search and submit resumes. I often got up earlier than I desired or burned the midnight oil to respond promptly.

Scriptural Encouragement: "There is a time for everything" (Eccles. 3:1).

HR Tip #4: Be Organized

A proactive person is organized! For instance, take time to set up an easy filing system—and I emphasize easy—that keeps you organized when you are responding to advertisements in the newspaper or journals.

What worked for me was cutting out the ad and stapling it to a photocopy of my cover letter. This way I had the what, when, and to whom of what I sent out for future reference. I kept these letters in a file folder by my computer. When someone called about a potential job, I could get my folder out, refer to it, and make notes on the back of the letter if necessary. Having the ad handy helped me ask good questions and answer the potential employer's questions too. My system couldn't have been simpler, yet it helped me stay organized.

Scriptural Encouragement: "Get wisdom, discipline and understanding" (Prov. 23:23).

HR Tip #5: Be Committed

A proactive person is committed! Few people like the commitment it takes to network. This is an area I have to stretch myself in because it makes me feel very vulnerable and as though I'm asking for help (which I am doing). But over and over again, I've seen doors opened because someone knew someone who needed someone with your exact skills. I've also found that most people like helping others, especially other likeable people.

Networking done respectfully and with integrity is an excellent opportunity to develop new relationships or build upon old ones. For the believer, networking can be a great opportunity to build relationships and share your testimony of what Christ is doing in your life, all at the same time. However you approach networking, never compel someone to help you. Helping should always be their choice.

Scriptural Encouragement: "Commit to the LORD whatever you do, and your plans will succeed" (Prov. 23:23).

HR Tip #6: Be Considerate

A proactive person is considerate! Always demonstrate your consideration through a follow-up telephone call, correspondence, or invitation to get together in the future as appreciation for the person's time. As follow-up to an interview or business prospect, always send a thank-you note or letter out that day or within the following days indicating your excitement about the company's vision and the possibilities of working for them.

And lastly, a professionally considerate person follows up on all leads, even those that don't appear too promising. This is just another way of letting the person who gave you the lead know that you appreciate her efforts enough to have followed this lead through. Unfortunately, I know people don't always do this because it's happened to me in the past: A friend is given a lead about a job but fails to follow up, lets one week turn into three, and then finally forgets about the lead until she sees you again or the lead is cold.

If we say "Thank you!" let's keep our word as Christians through our actions.

Scriptural Encouragement: "A man finds joy in giving an apt reply—and how good is a timely word!" (Prov. 15:23).

HR Tip #7: Be Exceptional

A proactive person is exceptional! Interviewing is the area for which you should be most proactive and prepared so that you stand out as exceptional. Discussing "why you are qualified" can be a bit unnerving; that's normal. Yet there are some interviewing strategies you can implement to have a successful meeting.

The more information you receive about the company (its mission, philosophy, and vision), the better your questions and the greater your understanding will be. Get on the Internet and do a little research prior to your interview, or better yet establish personal contact by calling the receptionist and asking for the company's brochure or other relevant literature. After you've done your research, begin formulating your answers to potential interview questions.

Learning to be a proactive listener is of utmost importance. Aside from your actual work-related abilities, this will be your greatest personal asset during the interview. For instance, if the interviewer tells you, "I'm looking for a detail-oriented person who can work independently, quickly, and with little supervision," and then asks, "What job traits do you think would make you an ideal candidate for this position?" your response should mirror what was just stated, but in your own words. Words like "self-starter," "detail-oriented," and "quick thinker," should immediately come to mind. However, having interviewed hundreds of candidates I'm surprised at how unprepared for questions like this people seem despite the fact they think they are "perfect for the job."

Being exceptional only requires the willingness to be proactive and take the extra effort with the information you are given.

Scriptural Encouragement: "Teach me knowledge and good judgment" (Ps. 119:66).

In sum, being proactive means doing some things before the process of change begins. God will provide the change in your life; however, you must become a proactive channel for this change to occur.

It's not enough to read the paper week after week or let information sit in your computer if you aren't responding in a timely manner, staying on top of things, following up on leads, or doing the necessary legwork to land that "perfect" job. You must seek God, devise a plan, and then be committed to following that plan through until God opens the door for the new opportunity you so desire.

The future is yours to take hold of. You can be like the majestic trees of Lebanon that David spoke of in Psalm 92:12–13, planted in the house of the Lord and flourishing in the courts of God, or be like the withering branch that bears no fruit because you are set on doing things your own way (John 15:6). The choice is yours; however, I pray that you will take time to seek the Lord and get prepared for the new places he desires to bring you into. He's waiting!

Waiting Is Not in Vain

You've done everything you should, could, and would, but still nothing! The reality of this process has caused a wave of emotional, spiritual, and professional self-reflection—to say nothing of insecurity.

The job process can be grueling to the point of making you feel like the life is being sucked out of you, but as sure as you are reading this book, God has a plan for your life as a believer. Victory is yours—but as a direct result of praise, prayer, and perseverance.

Praise While You Wait

God is always worthy of praise simply because each and every single day, every moment of a moment, he is God. Awesome, great, and mighty is he! Our praise must not stem from the things God can do for us but from the intimacy that comes from the privilege of knowing him.

When my husband and I first started talking about his retirement from the army, we began praying for favor and new opportunities as he transitioned from a military career to "civilian life." What we were doing was scriptural; however, I vividly remember God speaking to my heart and saying, "I've heard your prayers; now start praising me."

"Okay!" I thought, and from that moment on I began praising God for who he is: my provider (all my needs are being met), my protector (my heart is protected from the lies of the enemy), and my provision (I'm strengthened when it seems natural to give up).

Seven months later my husband was without a job, yet I continued to praise him because "The LORD is my strength and my song, he has become my salvation" (Ps. 118:14).

Salvation comes from the Hebrew word *yasa* meaning to "save, rescue, help, deliver, preserve, give victory. Initially used in the sense of rescuing people from national or individual crisis."[2] When I dwell on God's truth that he is victory, deliverance, and salvation, praising him becomes an expression of my faith in spite of my circumstances.

Often when I am tempted to become worrisome, the Holy Spirit quickens my heart and brings truth to my heart by saying, "Praise him, praise him, praise him!" "For great is the LORD and most worthy of praise. . . . Splendor and majesty are before him; strength and joy in his dwelling place. . . . Ascribe to the LORD glory and strength, ascribe to the LORD the glory due his name" (1 Chron. 16:25, 27–29).

Praying While Waiting

Throughout the process of writing this book I've been praying specifically for you. Yes, you are right, I don't know you by name. But the God I'm praying to created you and knew you'd be reading this book right now. He knows you by name even though I don't and may never. So as I prayed, "Lord, bless the women who will read this book; change their lives because of your truth, power, and might," I did so believing that he would bring this book into print just for you.

Similarly, I'm praying for my husband's coworkers even though "nothing" seems to be on the horizon for a job. I'm not going to let that stop me. I continue to pray for those he'll be working with and anticipating God's plan. When we say we trust God, we must direct our prayers accordingly. It would be foolish for me to say I believe God has a job for

Kevin but not render prayers for where he will work. Don't you agree?

We must be wise in our petitions to our Lord and Savior. How much better would it be for you and your future coworkers if this special and set apart place of ministry called work had been covered in prayers?

Our future workplaces can be radically transformed even before we get there. God has a purpose for you and your coworkers. Although you don't yet know what that is, you can use this time to pray that God would soften the hearts of your coworkers for the gospel of Jesus Christ. "No eye has seen, no ear has heard, no mind has conceived what God has prepared for those who love him" (1 Cor. 2:9).

Persevering during the Wait

God's promise says, "Let us not become weary in doing good, for at the proper time we will reap a harvest if we do not give up" (Gal. 6:9). The Greek word for time, *kairos*, means, "a period of opportunity. It is a critical or decisive point in time; a moment of great importance and significance; a point when something is ready or favorable."[3]

We are promised that at a critical time God will grant favor to us as evident through the harvest we reap. Continue to be patient with expectant joy. This is the true test of perseverance: being patient with a heart of expectancy and not one of murmuring, griping, and complaining. God's harvest is worth the wait, so don't allow yourself to settle for anything other than his best, especially when you are tempted to jump at the first "good" opportunity. For you know just as I do that not every "good" opportunity that arises is from God. Satan is clever and disguises himself as an angel of light, hoping to thwart God's plan for your life (2 Cor. 11:14).

Therefore, before accepting that job offer, seek God for his counsel again . . . and again and again until you have peace! Once you are given the "thumbs-up" from God, then by all means jump, shout, and respond affirmatively to the offer. But whatever you do, do not settle for anything but God's best!

"God is not unjust; he will not forget your work" (Heb. 6:10), so don't give up on the dreams, hopes, and aspirations he's placed in your heart. This waiting period isn't the time to forgo your goals but to press forward in achieving them. Expectantly wait on the Lord with joy. This is how you will be able to persevere.

Accepting a New Position

Brrringgg! "Hello, Ms. Wonderful! We are calling to extend you an offer of employment with our company. Can you start in two weeks?" *Two weeks?* you think, *How about yesterday?*

I can only rejoice in your excitement as you receive a call similar to this. Like you, I've waited with great anticipation for such a call and remember the sense of relief and exuberance when it actually came.

But before you hang up the phone, make certain you've had all your questions answered about the kind of benefits you can anticipate, the career opportunities available, and the overall work culture you will be part of. Let me illustrate my point by posing a question: Would you prefer a salaried position of $40,000 a year with mediocre benefits, little room for professional upward mobility, and a forty-five-hour-plus workweek, or a $38,000 a year salaried position with excellent benefits, great upward career mobility, and a flexible work environment? These are questions you have to answer before accepting an offer.

As someone who works best independently, work culture and management style play a crucial role in my overall sanity on the job. Therefore the last three jobs I had were great in the sense that I was given significant professional autonomy. In one case my boss worked in another state, and in the other two jobs my bosses traveled extensively. Salary was important but equally relevant was the management style of my boss, the work culture, and the overall benefits of the job.

In a nutshell, ask before accepting! But let me also say, "Congratulations! Praise God!" Am I being premature? Absolutely not! I'm just standing on God's Word with you: "'For I know the plans I have for you,' declares the LORD, 'plans to prosper you and not to harm you, plans to give you hope and a future'" (Jer. 29:11). Let God do the new thing in your life so that he may be glorified.

• • •

Personal Insight

What new truths has God revealed to you? How will you depend on the Holy Spirit so God's Word can be a light to your path? _____

_____

_____

_____

• • •

Spiritual Application

Write out the Scripture verse(s) in this chapter that gave you encouragement for your current work situation. _____

_____

_____

How is God speaking to you through this verse? _____

_____

_____

_____

What workplace actions will you commit to following through on as you strive to seek God before searching for the next opportunity? _____

_____

_____

_____

9

Celebrate His
Rich Blessings!

God's Transforming Power

May the LORD repay you for what you have done. May you
be richly rewarded by the LORD.

Ruth 2:12

Throughout our journey together we've discussed how
knowing your spiritual purpose for the workplace is
the key to resolutely living it out in your everyday decisions. I pray our time together has been invigorating for you.
Now it's time to celebrate the splendor of God's transforming power in our lives together.

Psalm 145:7 tells us to celebrate God's abundant goodness
and joyfully sing of his righteousness. Certainly we have much
to celebrate as Christians: his truths that transform us, his revelation that frees us, his provision that equips us, his goodness

that refines us, his compassion that uplifts us, his riches that he bestows on us, his Spirit who resides within us, and his Son who redeems us.

These extravagant gifts are abundantly more than we will ever be able to unwrap in a lifetime. How can we ever express our heartfelt gratitude to the giver of such rich and abundant blessings? As I contemplate this question I remember the woman I saw standing in the middle of a department store searching for the perfect gift to give to her father who has everything—and I realize that there is no perfect gift for our Father except our lives.

This is what this chapter is all about: celebrating God's indescribable gift through our lives! *To celebrate* is comparable to the word *to bless,* which means to honor or worship. As we seek to honor and worship God, let's revisit the life of Ruth and learn from her personal and work experiences. Then we will discuss celebrating God in our lives through tithing, fasting, balanced living, and thankfulness. Indeed this will be a time of celebration!

As we celebrate, honor, and bless the Lord we will experience him in even greater intimacy. The end result: being richly rewarded and blessed. If you are ready to bless the Lord and be blessed, then let's jump right in with our sister, friend, coworker, and mentor, Ruth.

Celebrate a Woman of God

Ruth knew how to celebrate God in her life with her life. At the beginning of the Book of Ruth, she was a woman peering into a bleak and grim future. She had no employment check, no pension, no status, and no home to call her own. Yet because of her faith in God, she went from having little to having much. God honored her with great riches and blessings, taking her on a spiritual, personal, and professional excursion she never could have imagined.

Not only did she succeed by the world's standards, but she attained what most of us are striving for today: to live out God's purpose in the workplace victoriously! No doubt if Ruth were alive today, she would be a frequent guest on various Christian and secular radio and television programs. I can just imagine the popular television host perching forward on the edge of her plush chair asking Ruth probing questions: "How did you climb the corporate ladder?" "How did you go from field laborer to great-grandmother of a king?" "What business tips would you offer today's career woman?"

Undoubtedly Ruth's response would be unexpected, because I believe she would redirect the conversation away from herself and use the opportunity to celebrate God in her life. It wouldn't surprise me one bit to see Ruth comfortably lean in close to the host as though she were about to confide a secret and say, "The key is *living for God, walking in his light,* and *respecting his authority!*" Then she would passionately start sharing heart to heart, woman to woman, about what it means to celebrate God in our lives.

This is my aim: I want our remaining time together to be like two women sharing heart to heart over a steaming cup of java (or tea if you prefer). So pull up your chair, get real close, and let's continue talking!

Living for God

Just as Ruth committed to living for God, as evident in her everyday decisions (see Ruth 1:16), we must commit to doing the same if we desire to celebrate God in our lives. She knew that the power of celebrating God in her life went beyond just knowing his purpose to living it out. She sacrificed the comforts of her life, her aspirations, and her dreams in order to obey God and follow his will. In essence she surrendered her nearsighted plans for God's limitless vision.

When we reflect on the decisions Ruth made, it seems almost ludicrous to imagine a Moabite woman serving the God of Israel, following her worn and tired mother-in-law into a foreign land, and seeking out employment opportunities in the field of a rich and highly respected landowner. The chances of these two women overcoming their dire circumstances seem very low. Yet because of Ruth's faith in God, she experiences him in a whole new way, changing the course of her life forever. In light of Ruth's willingness, I have to question my own obedience, especially as I seek to celebrate God in my life.

Few of us are willing to constantly die to self in order to obey God. Just think: When was the last time you put your personal desires for that promotion, salary increase, or new job on hold to follow God down an unfamiliar path? He asked Ruth, and she was no different than we are today.

Jesus lays the foundation for what it means to live for God when he says, "I tell you the truth, unless a kernel of wheat falls to the ground and dies, it remains only a single seed. But if it dies, it produces many seeds" (John 12:24). Ruth's life produced many good seeds because she honored God by living for him.

We all have areas in our lives that God requires us to die to so he can resurrect new life in us—the dying to self-indignation that keeps the seed of bitterness alive with coworkers; the dying to self-doubt that keeps the seed of fear alive, crippling God's purpose from going forward; the dying to self-deception that keeps the seed of pride and selfishness alive, tempting you to trust in self instead of God's Word; and of course, the dying to any area of your life that doesn't reflect God's truth in your life.

Ruth died to herself and lived for God. As a result she came to personally experience him as the Living God she could trust to meet her every need in the midst of overwhelming odds. The same God wants you to celebrate him in your life so you too can come to personally experience him as the Living God (Rev. 1:18).

Walking in His Light

I believe Ruth would also tell us to walk in God's light. She blessed the Lord by shining his light brightly before her mother-in-law, the harvesters, other coworkers, and Boaz (Ruth 2:2–9). Consider for a moment that some commentators believe Ruth was "the daughter of Eglon, king of Moab."[1] If this is the case, I have no doubt that Ruth could have pulled out her resume and begun spouting off a list of lofty credentials and reasons why she should be the manager of the harvesters instead of one of the harvesters.

Quite frankly, I believe this would have been my tactic, especially since I tend to have a "why follow when you know you can lead?" mentality. But not our Ruth! When we celebrate God's light in our lives, our words, actions, and deeds become dramatically different than what the world anticipates. Jesus tells us, "You are the light of the world. . . . let your light shine before men, that they may see your good deeds and praise your Father in heaven" (Matt. 5:14, 16). In other words, his light in us should give guidance and become the standard for those living in darkness.

Ruth celebrated God's light in her life through the simple things she did, like demonstrating humility and even simply saying "please" (Ruth 2:7). Think back to the last time you said "please" or voluntarily let another coworker get in front of you on the elevator, in the cafeteria line, or in the parking lot, especially when you were in a hurry. Letting his light shine in the workplace like Ruth did is a real celebration of God in our lives.

Ruth walked in God's light and came to personally experience him as the Light of the World upon whom she could depend to direct her path when letting her own light shine seemed most logical. The same God wants you to celebrate him in your life so you can personally experience him as the Light of the World (John 8:12).

Respecting His Authority

Finally, Ruth would tell us to respect God's authority in our lives. Once again, she celebrated God in her life by doing something many of our contemporaries (Christians included) would shake their heads at: "she bowed down with her face to the ground" out of respect when Boaz approached her (Ruth 2:10).

I don't believe God requires us to follow this example in the literal sense (unless we are in a country where this is customary); however, he is clear about the posture of respect we must maintain for those in authority over us. Bear in mind what the apostle Paul tells us in Titus 3:1–2: "Be subject to rulers and authorities . . . be ready to do whatever is good . . . show true humility toward all men."

Not showing up to work on time because your boss doesn't get to work on time is not respecting God's authority. If your workday begins at 8:00, then as a person celebrating God in your life you have a responsibility to show up on time. Ruth celebrated God in her life as she respected Boaz's authority over her. If you find it hard to respect your boss's authority, your boss will find it hard to respect God's authority in your life. Celebrating God in our lives means being profoundly different from our coworkers in both the big and small decisions to honor God's authority.

Ruth submitted to God's authority in her life and came to personally experience him as the Supreme Authority to whom she could willingly relinquish her control, knowing that even her earthly boss was subject to her heavenly boss's power and authority. The same God wants you to celebrate him in your life so you come to personally experience him as the Supreme Authority (Matt. 28:18).

Celebrate with Your Tithes

God declares a guilty verdict on anyone who doesn't bring tithes and offerings to him. He says in Malachi 3:8, "Will a man rob God? Yet you rob me. . . . in tithes and offerings." In this light, I'm guilty—a thief!

For years, as the pastor prayed I'd open my purse, rummage for my wallet, look for a couple of loose bills (preferably a five and a couple of ones), stuff the limp money into the offering envelope, and proudly wait for the offering basket. In the Book of Luke, Jesus rebukes the Pharisees for similar hypocrisy. They looked good on the outside because they followed all the right laws, but Jesus rebukes them as being "full of greed and wickedness" on the inside (Luke 11:39). They too were offering him their scraps disguised as tithes.

If we are to celebrate God in our lives, we must have pure hearts that seek to please the Lord with our giving. Often we give but dishonor God in our hearts because our motives are impure. In the Book of Malachi we see God's judgment on the Israelites because they let sin take root in their heart, turned their back on God's teachings, robbed him with their tithes and offerings, and then proudly walked in their wickedness (Mal. 3:7–8, 15).

Like the Israelites, I had an impure heart when it came to giving God his rightful tithe. Just as the giving was detestable to God during the times of Malachi, it is just as detestable today if we give grudgingly or with the wrong motives.

God wants our heart, not our money. His kingdom will not rise or fall based on our giving or not giving. Isaiah 66:1–2 says, "Heaven is my throne, and the earth is my footstool. . . . Has not my hand made all these things?"

What we give back to the Lord must be done as an act of celebration and worship to him. In the New Testament we read of the poor widow who generously and earnestly gave two coins and was more highly esteemed by Jesus than the rich people who were giving for recognition. Because her heart was pure and she "put in everything—all she had to live on" (Mark 12:44), Jesus considered her little to be much!

In the story of Ananias and Sapphira, told in Acts 5, we see a totally different picture. Here a husband and wife agree to sell a piece of property to help other church members. Yet when they return to the apostles, they falsely present a portion of their proceeds as if it were the total sum. The disciple Peter sees through the deception and says, "How is it that Satan has so filled your heart that you have lied to the Holy Spirit and have kept for yourself some of the money you received for the land? . . . You have not lied to men but to God" (Acts 5:3–4). The couple was struck down and died.

This was one of the first recorded sins of the New Testament church—the love of money—and therefore should warn us about the lures of greed. As you celebrate God in your life, be certain you aren't fabricating lies about giving in your mind to justify what's really in your heart. Had I followed what I knew to be truth, I would have joyfully given my tithes as another act of celebrating the Lord's plenty in my life. Second Corinthians 9:6–7 says, "Whoever sows sparingly will also reap sparingly, and whoever sows generously will also reap generously. Each man should give . . . not reluctantly or under compulsion, for God loves a cheerful giver." The best we can do is offer back to God what he's already given us.

As you celebrate God in your life with tithes and offerings, you will come to personally experience him as the God of Blessings. Malachi 3:10 says, "Bring the whole tithe into the storehouse. . . . Test me in this and see if I will not throw open the floodgates of heaven and pour out so much blessing that you will not have room enough for it."

Celebrate with Times of Fasting

Dr. Bill Bright, founder of Campus Crusade for Christ, says, "Fasting and prayer is a spiritual atomic bomb in its potential power."[2] When I first read this powerful word picture my heart pounded with excitement because the idea succinctly expressed my passion about the celebration of fasting and prayer.

Fasting and prayer was part of my Christian life as a teenager. But as I entered college, my commitment wavered, and for the following fifteen years I fasted intermittently, sometimes going years without seeking God in this way.

Finally, when my family lived on a military post in Kansas, I seriously heeded the Holy Spirit's prompting to reestablish this celebration. As I opened my heart to God's leading, he began placing other Christians who had such a passion in my pathway. Two such Christian women were my friends Chloe and Lisa. As these women shared heart to heart, God used them to begin revealing his truths to me about fasting and prayer. I began studying the people in both the Old and New Testaments who hungered after God and how fasting and prayer transformed their lives. As I read their personal stories,

I knew that God was taking me on a new pursuit of him and eagerly anticipated his truth maturing in my life from that moment on.

Consider the lives of Moses and Mordecai, whose lives were radically changed through fasting and prayer. Moses fasted for forty days and forty nights. During this time God revealed himself to Moses and gave him the new stone tablets on which the Ten Commandments were written again. Moses came to know and experience him as the God of Revelation and Restoration (see Exodus 34).

Mordecai fasted for three days and nights interceding for Queen Esther and his people, the Jews. Mordecai sought the God of refuge and saw him deliver a nation and thwart the schemes to annihilate his chosen people. Queen Esther, Mordecai, and a nation of people came to know and experience him as the God of Deliverance and Favor (see Esther 4).

Lest we minimize the importance of fasting, let's look to our Lord and Savior, Jesus Christ. We know he fasted for forty days and forty nights in the wilderness. During this period Satan tempted Jesus three separate times. As Jesus spent time in his Father's presence, he came to know and experience God as the Bread of Life, the Protector, and the One True God (see Matthew 4).

Lastly I draw your attention to Paul (also called Saul) and Barnabas, two Christian men who sought God's will through fasting and prayer before they journeyed on their first missionary trip to spread the gospel. As these disciples spent time worshiping, fasting, and praying, they came to know and experience God as the Good Shepherd and the Good News (see Acts 13).

If you desire to seek God in this way, let me encourage you to FAST: *Feast* on his Word, *Accept* his leading, *Start* with prayer, and *Trust* in his power and provision.

174

Feast on His Word

There's no better place to seek God than through his personal love letters found in the Bible. Fasting isn't a contest or a display of how spiritual you are. It is about feasting on God's truth. Jesus said, "I am the bread of life. He who comes to me will never go hungry, and he who believes in me will never be thirsty" (John 6:35).

No matter what others around you are doing or telling you, always seek God's Word before you begin a fast. Just as a long distance runner has to prepare ahead of time for the big race, you need time in the Word to prepare emotionally, spiritually, and physically.

Experiencing God up close and personal, being humbled before him, and then doing what he directs you to do is the key to fasting. This time in the Word and in prayer will result in "increased faith and trust in God and His Sovereign will."[3]

Accept His Leading

After you've been in the Word and in prayer about God's will, you may feel that this isn't the time for a fast. God may be saying, "Wait child, wait!" This happened to me, and as much as I wanted to move forward, I had to wait.

Fasting is about accepting his leading, no matter where it takes you. I have a dear girlfriend who loves the Lord, but when God directed her to a specific type of fast, she let reason convince her to run from where God was leading her. As a direct result of her disobedience, she abandoned her opportunity to celebrate God in her life through fasting.

When she did this she shifted the focus from God to self. Just like my friend, we must be careful not to shift our focus from God but rather celebrate him in our lives by accepting his leading.

Start with Prayer

Always start your fast with prayer, continue your fast in prayer, and end your fast in prayer. Or to put it even more simply, "pray continually" (1 Thess. 5:17). You will never go wrong this way.

Let's say you are fasting from lunch but instead of using this time to be in the Word, in prayer, or in worship, you run errands. If your heart's desire is to pursue the Creator and you yearn to know him more intimately, you need to be in his presence to hear what he's saying to you. This is where your life will be transformed; otherwise "fasting" from lunch without seeking God just becomes skipping lunch! Praying and fasting go hand in hand.

Trust His Power and Provision

Attempting to complete a fast of any kind will require that you base your resolve in Christ's power and provision and not in your own will or strength. Fasting requires dying to self so God can refine and purify us from the sin that reigns in our lives. In essence our fasting should draw us closer to the one who can create in us a pure heart (Ps. 51:10). And when we fast we must trust that this is what he is doing in and through us. Trusting in God's power and provision brings emotional, spiritual, and physical refuge.

God wants to be glorified through our fast so that our lives are changed and the lives around us are being directly impacted because of our time in his presence. If fasting isn't done as an act of celebration to know God's heart, then it will be power-

176

less and harvest no change. Our heart must be for God and on God. Fasting is never a way to try to manipulate our situation or God's will. King David attempted to manipulate his situation and change God's mind by fasting, but his efforts were futile. Once God declared judgment on David's sin, David could do nothing except repent (see 2 Sam. 12:15–19). In his case fasting was unavailing, as it will be for us if the desire of our hearts isn't to honor God.

Celebrate God in your life as you feast on his Word, accept where he's leading you, start your time in prayer, and trust in his power and provision for you. Come to intimately know and personally experience him as God, the Revelation, Deliverer, Bread of Life, Protector, Good Shepherd, Good News, the One True God!

Celebrate with Balanced Living

As Kendra Smiley wrote, "Look around you and be distressed, look within you and be depressed. Look to Jesus and be at rest."[4] What great encouragement and insight! Now if we could just heed this counsel when striving to maintain some balance in our overworked, overstressed, and oversaturated lives.

As a young girl I eagerly stood in line wearing my gym outfit in hopes of defying the balance beam. I would place my feet on the grainy blonde beam, hold my arms straight out, maintain my posture for a moment, and then gingerly place one foot in front of the other . . . hoping all the while to make it to the end without losing my balance.

That reminds me of my life today, except instead of taking one step at a time, I am on the balance beam attempting leaps and bounds. Sound familiar? It's difficult enough to maintain balance when it's only you on the balance beam—try adding a husband, children, church, chores, committees, and of course work. No wonder most of us feel like the main act in a circus show!

Even in the midst of our one-woman circus acts, we can have hope. Lamentations 3:22–24 says, "Because of the LORD's great love we are not consumed, for his compassions never fail. They are new every morning; great is your faithfulness. I say to myself, 'The LORD is my portion; therefore I will wait for him.'" As I juggled life's many responsibilities, I wrapped my arms around this verse and clung to it. If we are to celebrate God in our lives, we must bring balance into our lives.

Let's face it, bringing balance into our lives is no easy under-taking, especially if you are a person who likes to be in con-trol, like me, or someone who associates her value with what she is doing. Both personality types tend to continue taking on more responsibilities that contribute to an unnecessarily chaotic and hectic lifestyle.

If you find yourself doing lots of things but have little or no time to spend in God's Word or in prayer, then most likely you are being consumed with activity and not celebrating God in your life. God has given us his commitment of faithfulness, as we see in Lamentations; however, we must be willing to expe-rience him as our portion. This is the first step toward balance. If we believe God is our portion—our peace when we feel rest-less, our joy when we are down, our comfort when we are dis-traught, and our love when we feel unloved—then we must embrace his truth and trust that he really is our "enough"!

We must also learn to wait on him. Learn to wait for his blessings. Being busy without God's blessing is working in vain and against his will. I've found that when I'm anxiously wanting to get busy and do something, it's most often a direct result of imbalance in my life and looking for that next "high" in the thing I'm about to take on. If I really want to celebrate God in my life, I should be seeking my next "high" by spending more time in his presence waiting instead of doing.

Balance means coming to know that his divine power gives us everything—and I mean everything—that we need for life (2 Peter 1:3). Granted, celebrating balance in your life will most likely look different to you than it does for me; however, it will always look the same to God—abiding with him.

Before making another commitment (even church related), ask yourself the following three questions:

1. *Is this the best time?* Consider whether this commitment is for the present time or for the future.

2. *Does this need my involvement?* Consider whether your involvement is needed for this project to be successful.

3. *Will this glorify God or me?* Consider whether this will unequivocally bring glory to God or to you.

Celebrate God in your life through balanced living and come to know him as your portion.

Thank God It's Monday!

You're just about finished reading this book; you've taken notes and prayerfully committed to pursuing your purpose for the workplace; yet you still are living for Friday. What then?

I recently read a quote by an unknown author that said, "Exercise daily! Walk with the Lord." This is my encouragement to you, from one woman who struggles to maintain exercise as part of her own life. I know that if I want to get the maximum output from my body I must consistently exercise, eat well, and get a good night's sleep. Yet almost daily I fight against the desire to stay in bed just one more minute (which invariably turns into thirty minutes), avoid exercise, overeat, or stay up too late.

In the same way, we must fight against the desire to live like the world, embracing its lifestyle and ambitions. We are not to be conformed to this world but rather transformed by the renewing of our minds (Rom. 12:2). God is continually creating in you new life so you can experience him residing in you, others can see his life in you, and he can be exalted through you. It's all about that daily exercise: walking day by day with God. Words on the page may excite and encourage you today, but only by celebrating him will you experience his transforming power.

Celebrating "TGIM" in the workplace is radical because it means holding on to God's Word, declaring his Word, living out his Word, standing on his Word, and obeying his Word. This road you are journeying on is decidedly the road less traveled, even by other believers. The power is not in TGIM or even in your resolve. The power comes from the power source himself—God! As Revelation 19:1 says, "glory and power belong to our God." His power is what gives you significance, value, and purpose in the workplace. As Henry T. Blackaby and Richard Blackaby wrote in *Experiencing God Day-by-Day,* "It is God's desire that anywhere there is a Christian, God has a way for people to learn of His salvation (Rom. 10:14–15). Whenever an unbeliever meets a Christian, the unbeliever ought to be face to face with everything he needs to know in order to follow Christ. Our lives ought to be a highway of holiness, providing an easy access to God for anyone around us who seeks Him."[5]

Let's follow Jesus' example and bring glory to the Father by completing the work he's called us to do on earth (John 17:4). Ruth did and so can we. I am amazed and humbled to know that she never could have charted her destiny the way

God meticulously and miraculously orchestrated it. To the onlooker she was just a desperate foreigner looking for employment. But to God she was a woman willing to celebrate him in her life, and he was able to use her life to bring forth his life.

"Thanks be to God! He gives us victory through our Lord Jesus Christ" (1 Cor. 15:57). Now that's worth celebrating! Thank God It's Monday!

• • •

Personal Insight

What new truths has God revealed to you? How will you depend on the Holy Spirit so you can really know what it means to celebrate God in your life?_____

_____

_____

_____

• • •

Spiritual Application

Write out the Scripture verse(s) in this chapter that gave you encouragement for your current work situation. _____

_____

_____

_____

How is God speaking to you through this verse? _____

_____

_____

_____

What workplace actions will you commit to following through on as you strive to victoriously celebrate your workweek because of Jesus Christ in your life? _____

_____

_____

_____

Employee Resource Terms

New Definitions for the Christian in Today's Workplace

1. Chief Executive Officer: The Creator of the universe and author of truth.

2. Christian Employee: An ambassador for Jesus Christ.

3. Colleague: A coworker Christ died for.

4. Compensation: Undeserved benefits given from the CEO to an employee.

5. Conflict Management: Trusting God in all circumstances.

6. Conflict Resolution: The ability to forgive an offense.

7. Corporate Philosophy: Love thy neighbor.

8. Defamation: Dishonoring Jesus Christ in the workplace through your behavior.

9. Discrimination: Attempting to decide who is and who isn't worthy of God's love or forgiveness.

10. Diversity Training: What Jesus instituted when he chose the twelve disciples.

11. Documentation: A journal to report answered prayers.

12. Employee: Someone committed to being a beacon of God's light in the workplace.

13. Employee Conflict: Wavering between serving God and living for the world.

14. Employee Manual: The Bible.

15. Employee Wellness Program: Time in the Word, needed for maintaining wellness.

16. Empowerment: The Holy Spirit working in an employee, enabling success.

17. Equal Employment Opportunity: A covenant made by the CEO that all people will be given the same opportunities to serve him regardless of sex, age, race, or religion.

18. Executive Orders: Orders issued by CEO that must be followed (see Salvation).

19. Fitness Program: Walking with the Lord daily to maintain balance.

20. Formal Grievance Process: Going to the CEO to resolve spiritual warfare at work.

21. Freedom of Speech: The freedom to pray before speaking.

22. Holiday: Paid day to celebrate Christ (Christmas, Good Friday, Easter, etc.).

23. Hostile Work Environment: Satan's schemes in the workplace.

24. Job Description: Fulfilling the Great Commission in the workplace.

25. Life Insurance: A binding contract between you and Jesus Christ for all eternity.

26. Lunch Break: Fasting from a meal to pray and seek God.

27. Mediation: What Jesus Christ did on the cross and by his resurrection.

28. Misconduct: Behavior contrary to God's character and will.

29. Mission Statement: To seek and save the lost.

30. New Hire: When an employee accepts Christ into his or her life.

31. Part-time Employee: An employee who only shows up on Sundays.

32. Performance Review: God's stamp of approval on your life.

33. Proactive: An employee who's always ready to spread the gospel.

34. Promotion: When God moves an employee to another level spiritually.

35. Qualifications: Grace unwrapped in everyday life.

36. Recruiter: The Holy Spirit.

37. Rehabilitation Program: Repenting and receiving the Lord's forgiveness.

38. Retirement Package: Extravagant benefits given at retirement.

39. Salvation: Accepting Jesus Christ in your life.

40. Satan: A disgruntled former employee; the father of lies and deception.

41. Stress Management: Relying on God's strength, power, and presence.

42. Success: Accomplishing God's will and purpose for your life.

43. Tax-Free Contribution: Tithes and offerings freely given to the Lord.

44. Termination: Dying without life insurance (see Life Insurance).

45. Time Management: Being a good steward of God's time.

46. Training and Development: A lifelong training program for Christians.

47. Values: Principles based on Scripture that are displayed through behavior.

48. Willful Violation: Intentionally disobeying God's Word.

49. Workplace: Your mission field to proclaim the gospel.

50. Workplace Hazards: Obstacles the devil tries to place in the way of a Christian.

Notes

Chapter 1

1. I have followed the NIV translation's use of small capital letters for "I AM" where it is a translation of the Hebrew *Yahweh*.

2. Robert J. Morgan, *Nelson's Complete Book of Stories, Illustrations and Quotes* (Nashville: Thomas Nelson, 2000), 271.

3. *Random House College Dictionary*, rev. ed. (New York: Random House, 1988), 1502.

Chapter 2

1. Robert J. Morgan, *Nelson's Complete Book of Stories, Illustrations and Quotes* (Nashville: Thomas Nelson, 2000), 800.

Chapter 3

1. Lanson Ross, *Total Life Prosperity* (Wheaton: Tyndale House, 1982), 133.

2. Brian L. Harbour, *Living the New Testament Faith: James* (Nashville: Broadman & Holman, 1992), 66.

Chapter 4

1. Oswald Chambers, *My Utmost for His Highest: The Classic Edition* (Uhrichsville, Ohio: Barbour Publishing, Inc., 1935), May 26.

2. Francis Frangipane, *Holiness, Truth and the Presence of God* (Cedar Rapids, Iowa: Arrow Publications), 24.

3. *The New Webster's Comprehensive Dictionary of the English Language,* deluxe ed. (New York: Lexicon Publications, Inc., 1992), 797.

4. James Strong, *Strong's Hebrew and Greek Dictionaries,* 2d ed., electronic ed. (Cedar Rapids, Iowa: Parsons Technology, 1998).

5. Trent C. Butler, ed., *Holman Bible Dictionary,* electronic ed. (Cedar Rapids, Iowa: Parsons Technology, 1998).

Chapter 5

1. James Strong, *Strong's Hebrew and Greek Dictionaries,* 2d. ed., electronic ed. (Cedar Rapids, Iowa: Parsons Technology, 1998).

2. Adam Clarke, *Adam Clarke's Commentary on the New Testament,* electronic ed. (Cedar Rapids, Iowa: Parsons Technology, 1999).

3. Strong, *Strong's Hebrew and Greek Dictionaries.*

4. Ibid.

5. E. M. Bounds, *The Necessity of Prayer: Prayer and the Word of God,* electronic ed. (Cedar Rapids, Iowa: Parsons Technology, 1998).

Chapter 6

1. *The New Webster's Comprehensive Dictionary of the English Language,* deluxe ed. (New York: Lexicon Publications, Inc., 1992), 1132.

2. James Strong, *Strong's Hebrew and Greek Dictionaries,* 2d ed., electronic ed. (Cedar Rapids, Iowa: Parsons Technology, 1998).

3. Ibid.

4. Henry T. Blackaby and Richard Blackaby, *Experiencing God Day-By-Day: A Devotional and Journal* (Nashville: Broadman & Holman, 1997), 95.

5. Danny Lehmann, *Bringin' 'Em Back Alive: Reaching Your World for Jesus* (Springdale, Pa.: Whitaker House, 1987), 94.

Chapter 7

1. Spiros Zodhiates, *The Complete Word Study Dictionary: New Testament* (Chattanooga: AMG Publishers, 1992), 156.

2. Francis Frangipane, *Holiness, Truth and the Presence of God* (Cedar Rapids, Iowa: Arrow Publicatons, 1986), 112.

3. Albert Barnes, *Barnes' Notes on the New Testament,* electronic ed. (Cedar Rapids, Iowa: Parsons Technology, 1999).

Chapter 8

1. *The New Webster's Comprehensive Dictionary of the English Language,* deluxe ed. (New York: Lexicon Publications, Inc., 1992), 797.

2. *Hebrew-Greek Key Word Study Bible, New International Version* (Chattanooga: AMG Publishers, 1996), 1522.

3. Ibid., 1635.

Chapter 9

1. Adam Clarke, *Adam Clarke's Commentary on the Old Testament,* electronic ed., "Preface to the Book of Ruth" (Cedar Rapids, Iowa: Parsons Technology, 1999).

2. From the introduction to Ronnie W. Floyd's *The Power of Praying and Fasting: 10 Secrets of Spiritual Strength* (Nashville: Broadman & Holman, 1997), xii.

3. Ibid., 208.

4. Kendra Smiley, *Empowered by Choice: Positive Decisions Every Woman Can Make* (Ann Arbor, Mich.: Servant Publications, 1998), 63.

5. Henry T. Blackaby and Richard Blackaby, *Experiencing God Day-By-Day: A Devotional and Journal* (Nashville: Broadman & Holman, 1997), 190.

Kim Hackney is a wife, mother of three, and president and founder of Celebrating Victory, a ministry committed to encouraging believers to live victoriously in everyday life. Kim has worked in human resources management and consulting for over a decade and holds a master's degree in human resources. A Christian inspirational speaker and writer, she and her family reside in Cary, North Carolina. For more information on Kim's ministry, visit her web site, www.celebratingvictory.org.